BREAK AN EGG!

THE
BROADWAY
COOKBOOK

BREAK AN EGG!

THE
BROADWAY
COOKBOOK

FIFTY-FIVE RECIPES INSPIRED BY MUSICALS FROM *OKLAHOMA!* TO *HAMILTON*

TARA THEOHARIS

Photographs by Ted Thomas

Illustrations by Neryl Walker

INSIGHT
EDITIONS

SAN RAFAEL • LOS ANGELES • LONDON

PROGRAM

A Letter From the Director — 7

Preshow: Common Terms and Techniques — 8

Overture: Appetizers — 13

Egg Rolls for Mr. Goldstone	*Gypsy*	15
Clambake Codfish Chowder	*Carousel*	16
Waiting for the Egg	*1776*	18
Cheesy Street	*Annie*	20
Don't Fry for Me, Argentina	*Evita*	23
Plant Food	*Little Shop of Horrors*	24
Greens, Greens, Nothing but Greens	*Into the Woods*	25
Along Came Bialy	*The Producers*	26
Totally Shucked	*Spring Awakening*	28

Chorus Tunes: Sides and Condiments — 31

Ol' Man River Rolls	*Show Boat*	32
Too Darn Hot Sauce	*Kiss Me, Kate*	34
Professor Harold Dill	*The Music Man*	35
Tradition-al Challah	*Fiddler on the Roof*	37
A Sunny Ball of Butter	*Funny Girl*	40
I'm Still Schmear	*Follies*	43
I Yam What I Yam	*La Cage aux Folles*	44
The Internet Is for Corn	*Avenue Q*	45
Pain du 24601	*Les Misérables*	47
Lady Marmalade	*Moulin Rouge!*	48

Showstoppers: Entrées — 51

Schnitzel With Noodles	*The Sound of Music*	52
Gruel, Glorious Gruel	*Oliver!*	55
Turkey and Dumplings	*Hello, Dolly!*	56
Age of Asparagus	*Hair*	57
Mama's Well-Peppered Ragù	*Chicago*	59
Frank-N-Furter's Meat Loaf	*The Rocky Horror Show*	60
The Wurst Pies in London	*Sweeney Todd: The Demon Barber of Fleet Street*	62
Pasta With Meatless Balls	*Rent*	64
The King's Pastrami on Rye	*Newsies*	65
Newfoundland Toutons	*Come From Away*	67

Eleven O'Clock Number: Cocktails

69

Old-Fashioned Wedding — Annie Get Your Gun — 71
Another Vodka Stinger — Company — 72
Rum Tum Tonic — Cats — 73
The Amazing Technicolor Dream Throat — Joseph and the Amazing Technicolor Dreamcoat — 75

The Wizard and Ice — Wicked — 76
Cuban Milkshake — Guys and Dolls — 78
Sherry Baby — Jersey Boys — 79
The Most Beautiful Thing — Kinky Boots — 81
My Shot — Hamilton — 82
Sunshine on the Shelf — Hadestown — 85

Encore: Desserts

87

Laurey's Prize-Winning Tarts — Oklahoma! — 88
Señorita Lolita Banana Flambé — Damn Yankees — 90
Loverly Chocolate Truffles — My Fair Lady — 91
Officer Krupcakes — West Side Story — 92
Coffee Break Cake — How to Succeed in Business Without Really Trying — 94

A Pineapple Parfait for You — Cabaret — 96
Sandy Dees — Grease — 97
Angel (of Music) Food Cake — The Phantom of the Opera — 98
Honey, Honey — Mamma Mia — 103
Big, Beautiful Blondie — Hairspray — 104
Piragua, Piragua — In the Heights — 105
Spooky Mormon Hell Cream Donut — The Book of Mormon — 107
Sugar Daddy Honey Roll — Hedwig and the Angry Inch — 108
Pomatter Pie — Waitress — 110
A La Mode Sundae — Dear Evan Hansen — 112
Revenge Party Cake — Mean Girls — 115

Party Time!

119

Tony Awards Soirée — 120
Cast Party — 123
Prematinée Brunch — 124

Curtain Call: Acknowledgments

127

A LETTER FROM THE DIRECTOR

A great meal is like a great show—it leaves you satisfied, inspired, and thinking about it for days afterwards. The two experiences require the same ingredients, after all: a creator, a book, and a desire to make something great. If you love food and theater, you're in luck because this book is your ticket to creating delicious meals inspired by some of the most iconic and beloved productions in the business. Whether you're a novice or a seasoned home chef, we have something exciting for you. It could be a dish straight out of a show, such as Laurey's Prize-Winning Tarts (page 88), or something a little more inspired-by, such as the Angel (of Music) Food Cake (page 98). Either way, as long as you follow the directions, remember your blocking, and don't overdo the cheese, you should earn a standing ovation.

If you're new to the stage and feeling some opening-night nerves, give yourself a good warm-up by looking through Preshow: Common Terms and Techniques (page 8). It includes helpful techniques of the culinary trade plus definitions of some of the terms and ingredients you'll see throughout the book.

The recipes are organized according to their appropriate place in the program and then loosely by the year they first appeared on Broadway. Go straight to your favorite show, or flip through to discover something new. If you're an entertainer, be sure to check out our Party Time! chapter (page 119) for fun, easy suggestions for decorations, activities, and menus for three different Broadway-themed parties (using our show-inspired recipes, of course).

Like any good script, these recipes are an opportunity for you to flex your creativity. Once you feel comfortable with them, feel free to revise them to let your particular skills and tastes shine. Swap out the type of meat or vegetable. Add your favorite spice. Substitute ingredients to make them dairy-, gluten-, or alcohol-free. Your revival may go on to become even more celebrated than the original.

Finally, I'd like to say thank you for picking up this book. It has been a major passion project for me—one I've been dreaming about and planning for a long time. That there are others out there that love Broadway, cooking, and goofy puns as much as I do reminds me how great our theater community is and how lucky I am to be a part of it.

Now, go break an egg, kid. Just remember, no matter what happens: The stove must go on.

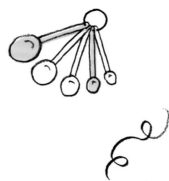

Preshow:
Common Terms
and Techniques

No need for professional training—you've got the talent in you already.

Anyone can cook. Really! But before you open the fridge or turn on the stove, take your time, read the recipe thoroughly, and look up anything you don't know. It might take a little longer the first time you walk through a recipe, but you'll be a star before you know it.

READ THE SCRIPT

You don't need to be off book, but you should read the recipe and know your blocking before you begin cooking. No one ever gives their best performance in a cold read, after all.

PLACES, EVERYONE!

You set your props and costumes before going onstage, and you do the same in the kitchen. You may have heard of the French phrase *mise en place*. It describes the act of prepping all your ingredients and tools before you start to cook—and it is a key part of any star cook's success. By pulling everything you need out of the pantry and fridge, making sure you have the right pans and baking sheets, and chopping your ingredients in advance, you'll avoid forgetting a prop or forcing an impromptu quick change while the soup's on. No one wants that.

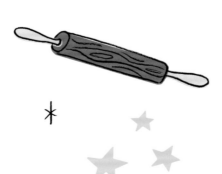

TOOLS OF THE TRADE

These tools and techniques will help you give your best performance night after night.

CRUMB COAT

Icing a cake is like painting a backdrop. It needs a primer: something to create a smooth surface for the icing. That's where a crumb coat comes in. A crumb coat is a thin layer of frosting you spread over a cake before fully frosting it. It catches crumbs that may have otherwise ended up in the frosting, creating a clean canvas for your frosting art.

CUTTING IN BUTTER

When you're asked to cut butter into flour, you're being asked to add small chunks of cold butter to a flour mixture and then use a pastry blender or your hands to grind that butter into the flour until you have a uniform and fairly coarse mixture. If you're using your hands, I recommend grabbing and pinching the flour and butter together, rubbing the butter between your fingers to spread it throughout the flour. Keep grabbing and pinching handfuls of butter and flour until a dry, crumb-like mixture forms.

DOUBLE BOILER

A double boiler consists of two stacked pots or a pot with a metal bowl set on top. The bottom pot should contain about an inch of water (the water shouldn't touch the top pot). When placed over heat, the steam from the simmering water in the bottom pot will gently heat the contents in the pot above. Use a double boiler to melt chocolate and other sensitive ingredients without risking scorching them.

FLOATING

Some cocktail recipes may request that you float an ingredient. This means you slowly pour the ingredient over the back of a spoon. The float ingredient will layer on top of the ingredients already in the glass rather than mixing in.

FOLDING

Need to fold in an ingredient? Folding is just a careful method of mixing one thing into another. Add one item to the other, and slowly lift and turn one over the other like you're folding an omelet. Continue folding until the ingredients are thoroughly blended. Recipes will call for folding when an ingredient is fragile or when additional stirring would toughen the final product—often an issue with glutenous dishes.

FRUIT TWISTS

A fruit twist can be a beautiful addition to a cocktail, and they're surprisingly easy to make: Slice a thin round of fruit. Make a cut through one section of the rind, and peel or cut the full circle of rind away from the fruit. Twist the rind around your finger, and voila!

FRYING

Frying does not have to be scary, and it absolutely does not require any fancy appliances. All you need is a Dutch oven or other large, heavy pot. Fill the pot up a few inches with canola oil, and heat, covered, until the oil reaches your desired temperature. See Thermometers (page 10) for more information on finding the right thermometer for your needs.

JULIENNE

When a recipe says to julienne something (most often vegetables), it means to cut the ingredient into long, thin, matchstick-shaped pieces. These pieces are usually around 3 inches long and ⅛ inch thick. A julienned vegetable is thicker and more intentionally cut than a shredded vegetable.

MUDDLE

To muddle cocktail ingredients—often herbs, fruit, and sugar—press and grind the ingredients against the bottom of a shaker or glass to release their flavors. You muddle with a muddler, an inexpensive tool that can be found almost anywhere.

PASTRY BAGS AND TIPS

Want your cakes, cookies, and cupcakes to look like they came straight from the bakery? Get some pastry bags and pastry tips. Pastry tips come in a variety of sizes and shapes, but the most common are the ones with a large round hole or a large star-shaped opening. When you're ready to frost your cake, place the tip of your choice into the corner of a pastry bag. Cut off the excess corner until the pastry tip fits snug and peeks out of the bag. Next, fold out the top edge of the bag, making a small cuff, and then fill the bag with your icing or frosting. The cuff guarantees you'll have some unfilled space at the top by which to hold the bag. Once the bag is filled, gently press the frosting down toward the tip, twisting the top to prevent it from coming out when squeezed.

If you're in a pinch and don't have a pastry bag, a plain old zippered bag works too. Fill the bag with your frosting, and snip one of the corners off.

SEPARATING EGGS

When you need to separate the egg yolk from the egg white, crack an egg in the middle and carefully open it up over a bowl. Carefully shift the yolk back and forth from half shell to half shell, letting the egg white pour out into the bowl.

SHREDDING

Shredding creates long thin pieces of food that don't need to be uniform in size. Many grocery stores sell pre-shredded vegetables, but it's easy to shred them at home. For leafy vegetables like lettuce or cabbage, use a knife to cut thin strips. For carrots and other hard vegetables, peel the vegetable and then shred using a box grater's largest holes. For chicken and other meats, first cook the meat until tender (usually in liquid). Let cool and then shred by pulling the meat with two forks.

SHUCKING

Shucking an oyster can seem intimidating, but once you've practiced a few times, it will seem so simple. Use a kitchen towel to hold the oyster flat side up. Find the seam, and gently push an oyster knife or a butter knife into it. Slide the knife back and forth until the oyster pops open. Carefully slide the knife underneath the oyster to detach the meat from the shell, careful not to spill any of the "oyster liquor."

STAND MIXER

A stand mixer is a cook's best friend. Seriously. Especially for bread making and baking in general, a stand mixer is like a resident sous chef. Make sure yours has a standard mixer attachment, whisk attachment, and bread hook attachment.

THERMOMETERS

Frying, candy making, and cooking meat are all great opportunities for a thermometer. Having one nearby means you won't mess up your recipe—or risk getting anyone sick. Meat thermometers are great for meat, but candy thermometers should be used for candy and frying. Want to get really fancy? With an infrared thermometer, you can see the temperature just by pointing a light at an object, and you can use it for anything. Plus they're not much more expensive than the other options.

ZEST

Typically, you zest a citrus fruit by rubbing it over a zester or microplane to collect thin, small flakes of the peel. When a recipe calls for, say, a tablespoon of zest, that's what it means. But zest can also refer to larger, intact pieces of the outside (the colorful part) of a citrus peel. It adds a ton of flavor to any dish or drink.

INGREDIENTS FOR SUCCESS

A veteran performer's thoughts on some common ingredients you'll find in these recipes.

BUTTER

Pay attention to whether the recipe calls for salted or unsalted butter. In most cases, cooking recipes will use salted butter, while baking recipes will call for unsalted butter and added salt to give the baker more control over the amount of salt in the recipe.

FLOUR

Most of the recipes in this book use all-purpose flour, with a few exceptions that use bread flour, rye flour, or cornmeal. If you have a preferred alternative flour, you are welcome to substitute; be sure to pay attention to the substitution ratio.

FOOD COLORING

In baked goods and frostings, gel coloring works best. The colors are more vibrant and won't add extra liquid to your final product. For beverages, liquid food coloring works best.

PEARL DUST

Pearl dust is a very fine, shimmery ingredient for cake and cookie decorating. You can find it at most craft and baking stores, as well as online. Mix a small amou nt in drinks, or brush some on the tops of cookies and candies to add a bit of magic and flair that your friends won't expect.

SALT

These recipes were written and tested with kosher salt in mind. Kosher salt cooks and bakes very well, and it is milder in taste than iodized salt. Its flakes are also larger, making it easy to grab a pinch and more attractive for presentation. Some recipes call for sea salt flakes—these are slightly larger, though thinner, pieces of salt, perfect for sprinkling over a loaf of bread. Finally, the occasional recipe will call for rock salt, larger pieces of salt used for more utilitarian purposes—balancing oysters, melting ice, etc. This type of salt is not traditionally made for consumption.

VANILLA

Get yourself some good vanilla. Either pick up some real vanilla extract (skip the imitation stuff), or if you want to get real fancy, try vanilla bean paste. You can substitute extract for paste one-for-one. It's best when you really want to taste the vanilla flavor or when you're not baking the dish.

1

OVERTURE

APPETIZERS

• •

You're in your seat, full of anticipation, your ears picking up the sounds of instruments tuning. Suddenly, the lights dim and the overture begins, offering your senses their first taste of your musical adventure.

These appetizers serve as a tantalizing taste of what's to come, whetting the appetite and setting expectations for the rest of the meal. Have these prepared for guests to munch on while you're finishing meal preparations, or enjoy as a separate snack.

• •

Egg Rolls for Mr. Goldstone
Inspired by *Gypsy* (1959)

When a man walks into your room and offers you—whoops—your *children* a chance at stardom, you offer him whatever you have. And you could do a lot worse than an egg roll. Just remember this moment. Remember it after your children are grown and don't need you anymore. Remember to bring it up again in the middle of a really juicy nervous breakdown. And then? Go get yourself an egg roll, mama. It's your turn.

2 tablespoons peanut oil

4 cups shredded cabbage

1 cup shredded carrots

¾ cup minced scallions

½ cup bean sprouts

1 tablespoon minced ginger

2 cloves garlic, minced

1 teaspoon sugar

Salt and pepper, to taste

½ cup chicken stock

2 cups julienned or shredded Chinese barbeque or roasted pork

1 tablespoon soy sauce

1 tablespoon sesame oil

1 egg

12 egg roll wrappers

½ cup canola oil for frying

YIELD: 12 EGG ROLLS

1. Heat the peanut oil in a wok or large skillet over medium-high heat.
2. To make the filling mixture, add the cabbage, carrots, scallions, bean sprouts, ginger, and garlic. Cook for 2 to 3 minutes or until everything begins to soften. Add the sugar and season with salt and pepper. Add the chicken stock, pork, soy sauce, and sesame oil, and mix everything together. Cook until the stock is warmed, 1 to 2 minutes.
3. Pour the filling mixture into a colander to drain, and allow to cool.
4. Prep the egg wash: Beat an egg in a small bowl and set aside.
5. On a clean surface, lay out an egg roll wrapper with one corner pointing toward you. Spoon about ¼ cup of filling onto the middle of the wrapper. Then carefully fold the corner closest to you over the filling, and roll. When the egg roll is about halfway rolled up, fold in the side corners and continue rolling. Brush some of the egg wash on the last corner of the egg roll and seal tightly. Place on a baking sheet or large plate. Repeat until all the filling is gone.
6. Heat canola oil in your wok or large skillet to 350°F. Fry the egg rolls in small batches (don't fully crowd the pan) for 3 to 5 minutes each or until golden brown, moving them around often to make sure they get evenly browned on each side.
7. Place the cooked egg rolls on a paper towel–lined pan or plate until you've fried all of them.
8. Serve warm with duck sauce, sweet and sour sauce, hot mustard, or soy sauce.

Clambake
Codfish Chowder
Inspired by *Carousel* (1945)

When June starts bustin' out all over,
you know it's time to plan the annual
clambake. And no clambake is complete
without some nice chowder to hold you
over until the main course. Enjoy this
New England-style chowder with codfish,
onion, and bacon. It's fittin' for an
angel's choir!

4 ounces salt pork or bacon

2 tablespoons unsalted butter

1 large onion, halved vertically and cut in thin wedges

4 stalks celery, chopped

¼ teaspoon black pepper plus more to taste

½ teaspoon kosher salt plus more to taste

2 Yukon Gold potatoes, peeled and diced into ½-inch cubes

2 cups fish stock (or substitute chicken broth or clam juice)

1 tablespoon fresh thyme

1 bay leaf

1½ pounds skinless cod, cut into 2-inch chunks

1½ cups heavy whipping cream

Fresh flat-leaf parsley, chopped, for topping

Fresh chives, minced, for topping

YIELD: 4 SERVINGS

1. In a large Dutch oven or large, heavy pot, cook the salt pork or bacon over medium heat until browned but not fully crisp, about 8 minutes. Remove the salt pork to a paper towel–lined plate, leaving the grease in the pot. Once cool, crumble or cut the meat into small pieces for serving and set aside.

2. Add the butter, onion, celery, ¼ teaspoon pepper, and ½ teaspoon salt to the pot, and cook until the vegetables are softened, about 5 minutes.

3. Add the potatoes, stock, thyme, and bay leaf and bring to a boil. Reduce heat and simmer for 10 minutes or until potatoes are tender.

4. Add the cod, and cook for another 5 minutes or until the fish is opaque. Stir in the whipping cream, and simmer for 10 more minutes or until soup is creamy and the cod starts breaking into smaller pieces.

5. Remove the bay leaf and serve hot with a sprinkle of parsley, chives, bacon, salt, and pepper.

Waiting for the Egg

Inspired by *1776* (1969)

Remember that show about our founding fathers? The one that made kids everywhere excited about US history again? No, not *Hamilton* . . . we're talking about *1776*. While not quite as diverse, groundbreaking, or, well, *revolutionary* as *Hamilton*, *1776* still showed the human side of the people we read about in history books and gave us some insight into the creation of the Declaration of Independence.

In "Waiting for the Egg," Ben Franklin, Thomas Jefferson, and John Adams fight over what the official bird of America should be while musing on the metaphorical egg that is the new nation. In honor of Ben Franklin's vote, this traditional English breakfast features turkey in its grilled sandwich soldiers.

1 egg
1 tablespoon salted butter
2 slices white bread
Dijon mustard for spreading
1 ounce white cheddar cheese, shredded
1 ounce Gruyère cheese, shredded
1 thin slice turkey

YIELD: 1 SERVING

1. Fill a small saucepan with about 3 inches of water and boil over high heat.
2. Reduce the temperature to medium-high heat to maintain a light simmer. Using a slotted spoon or skimmer, carefully place the uncracked egg into the saucepan. Cook for 6 minutes to make a soft-boiled egg.
3. While the egg is cooking, make the soldiers. Butter one side of each slice of bread, and spread Dijon mustard on the other side of one slice. Put both bread slices in a large nonstick pan on medium-high heat, butter side down. Mix the cheddar and Gruyère cheeses together, and sprinkle half of the shredded cheese onto the bread without the mustard. Then top with the turkey slice. Sprinkle the rest of the cheese onto the turkey, and top with the other piece of bread, mustard side down. Press down on the sandwich with a spatula. Continue to cook, flipping occasionally, until both sides are golden brown and the cheese is melted (about 1-2 additional minutes per side). Cut the sandwich into thin strips.
4. Remove the egg pot from the stove when done, and run under cold water until you can remove the egg. Place in an egg cup or shot glass. Crack the top with a spoon or knife, remove the top of the shell, and season with salt and pepper. Dip the soldiers into the runny yolk and eat.

Cheesy Street

Inspired by *Annie* (1977)

While Miss Hannigan, her brother, and "that dumb hotel" are scheming their way to easy street, you can get yourself to cheesy street with this delicious "liquid-gold" fondue. It's fancy enough for Daddy Warbucks but so quick and easy that you'll be done before you can sing "Tomorrow." Bet your bottom dollar.

FONDUE

1 pound sharp cheddar cheese, shredded
1 tablespoon cornstarch
¼ teaspoon dry mustard
1 tablespoon butter
2 tablespoons chopped shallot
2 cloves garlic, minced
1 cup Sauvignon Blanc
⅛ teaspoon ground nutmeg

DIPPERS

Bread, cut into cubes
Apples, sliced
Small potatoes, roasted
Pretzels
Sausage, thickly sliced

YIELD: 4 SERVINGS

1. To make the fondue: Mix the cheese, cornstarch, and mustard in a medium bowl and set aside.
2. Melt the butter in a medium saucepot over medium heat. Add the shallot and garlic, and cook for two minutes or until softened.
3. Add the Sauvignon Blanc, and bring to a boil.
4. Turn the heat down to low, and add the cheddar mixture. Stir until the cheese is completely melted and blended with the other ingredients, about 90 seconds.
5. Place the pot on a trivet, or pour the contents into a fondue pot. Sprinkle the nutmeg on top.
6. Serve family style with the dippers: bread, apples, potatoes, pretzels, sausage, and anything else you fancy.

TIP

Don't want to go full Hannigan? Make your fondue less boozy by substituting 1 cup vegetable broth and 1 tablespoon lemon juice for the Sauvignon Blanc.

Don't Fry for Me, Argentina
Inspired by *Evita* (1979)

In *Evita*, Eva Perón works her way up the political ladder only to reassure her supporters that she is still one of them in a legendary power ballad that is the ambition of every budding diva in the biz. While Eva was able to convince her *descamisados* that she had their best interests at heart, she might have been even more successful had she tossed some of these Argentinian empanadas down to the starving crowd. These tasty treats are warm, hearty, and delicious, whether you fry them or not. Now that's something everyone can get behind.

DOUGH
3 cups all-purpose flour
1 teaspoon kosher salt
½ cup cold salted butter
¾ cup water

FILLING
2 tablespoons salted butter
1 white onion, diced
1 red pepper, diced
1 pound lean ground beef
2 tablespoons paprika
1 tablespoon ground cumin
1 teaspoon kosher salt
½ teaspoon cayenne pepper
½ teaspoon black pepper
¼ cup sliced green olives
2 hard-boiled eggs, chopped
Canola oil for frying

YIELD: 12 EMPANADAS

1. To make the dough: Mix the flour and salt together in a large bowl. Cut in the butter (page 9), and mix thoroughly with a pastry blender or your hands. Add in water 1 tablespoon at a time, mixing between each addition. Once the dough is fully mixed, flatten it into a disc, cover with plastic wrap, and refrigerate while you prep the meat, or for approximately 30 minutes.
2. To make the filling: Melt the butter in a large sauté pan on medium heat, and add the onion and red pepper. Cook until onions are translucent and pepper is softened, 3 to 5 minutes.
3. Add ground beef, paprika, cumin, salt, cayenne, and black pepper to the pan, and cook until browned, about 8 minutes, stirring often.
4. Let the beef mixture cool slightly, then mix in the olives and eggs.
5. Take the dough out of the refrigerator, and divide into 12 equal sections. Roll each section into a golf ball–sized ball, flatten with your palm, and then use a rolling pin to roll into a 5-inch circle.
6. Place 2 heaping tablespoons of the meat mixture into the center of each circle, and fold the circles in half. Pinch the edges together well to keep the meat sealed in.
7. Pour about 3 inches of canola oil into a large, deep pot, and bring to a boil. Place a few empanadas at a time (try to avoid crowding) into the hot oil for 5 minutes, turning once. Rest on a paper towel to soak up excess oil.

TIP

Don't fry—you can make a delicious baked version of the empanadas if you prefer. Just bake at 400°F for 20 minutes or until light golden brown.

Plant Food

Inspired By *Little Shop of Horrors* (2003)

Poor Seymour. He just wants his strange new plant to grow—but he didn't expect it to prefer human blood to fertilizer. Channel your inner Audrey II with these finger-shaped mozzarella cheese sticks oozing with "bloody" marinara sauce. They'll have you screaming, "Feed me!"

2 cups marinara sauce
12 thin slices mozzarella cheese
1 cup all-purpose flour
3 eggs
3 tablespoons whole milk
2 cups panko breadcrumbs
1 teaspoon garlic powder
1 teaspoon dried parsley
1 teaspoon dried oregano
1 teaspoon dried basil
1 teaspoon kosher salt
½ teaspoon black pepper
Canola oil for frying

YIELD: 12 MOZZARELLA STICKS

1. Pour the marinara sauce into tube-shaped ice cube trays or thick straws. Freeze for 1 hour or until completely frozen.
2. Warm the cheese slices in the microwave for about 10 seconds, just to soften them.
3. Remove the sauce tubes, and wrap one slice of cheese around them each. Place the cheese sticks back in the freezer seam-side down while you prepare the dipping stations for breading the cheese sticks.
4. Place the flour on a large plate. Whisk together the eggs and milk in a bowl. On another large plate, mix the breadcrumbs and spices together.
5. Pull the cheese sticks out of the freezer. Working one at a time, dredge each in flour, dip in the egg mixture, and then roll in the breadcrumbs. Dip each breaded cheese stick in the egg once more, and then roll in breadcrumbs again.
6. Freeze the cheese sticks for 30 minutes.
7. Fill a large, heavy pot at least 2 inches up with canola oil, and heat over medium-high heat until temperature is between 350° and 375°F.
8. Add the breaded cheese sticks to the oil (be careful not to overcrowd), and cook while rotating carefully for 2 minutes or until golden brown on all sides.
9. Let drain and cool slightly on a plate covered with paper towels.

Greens, Greens, Nothing but Greens

Inspired by *Into the Woods* (1987)

We all know the witch can be a bit protective of her produce, but we also know that eating nothing but greens can get old after a while. Let's imagine a world where she's willing to share with her neighbors—they get some of her greens, she gets some bread from the bakery for croutons, and Milky White provides the milk for fresh cheese. Together they make a salad good enough to lift any curse.

THE BAKER'S CROUTONS

1 loaf day-old bread
¼ cup olive oil
1 teaspoon garlic salt
1 teaspoon kosher salt
½ teaspoon black pepper

SALAD

3 cups chopped green leaf lettuce
2 cups watercress
1 cup shredded cabbage
½ cup shaved asparagus
1 green pepper, julienned
½ cucumber, halved vertically and sliced
½ cup garbanzo beans
¼ cup sliced green onion
¼ cup crumbled feta

GREEN GODDESS DRESSING

1 avocado
1 cup water
½ cup sliced green onion
½ cup fresh basil
¼ cup fresh parsley
3 tablespoons apple cider vinegar
2 tablespoons lemon juice
2 tablespoons chopped onion
1 clove garlic, minced
¼ teaspoon kosher salt
⅛ teaspoon black pepper

YIELD: 8 SERVINGS

1. To make the croutons: Preheat the oven to 400°F, and cut the bread into ¾-inch cubes. Place the bread, olive oil, and seasonings in a large bowl and mix together. Spread the bread out in a single layer on a baking sheet, and bake for 10 to 15 minutes or until crisp and slightly browned, flipping halfway through.
2. To make the dressing: Combine all dressing ingredients in a blender or food processor, and blend until smooth. Set aside.
3. To make the salad: Toss together the lettuce, watercress, cabbage, asparagus, green pepper, cucumber, garbanzo beans, green onion, and ¼ cup dressing until everything is equally coated.
4. Top individual servings with croutons and crumbled feta.

TIP

Keep leftover dressing bottled in the fridge for up to a week.
This salad is very versatile. Meat eater? Add some chicken. Vegan? Remove the cheese. Add in any fresh greens or herbs you have from your garden. Just avoid stealing from your neighbor if you can.

Along Came Bialy

Inspired by *The Producers* (2001)

To raise money for the ultimate Broadway scam, you've got to seduce a lot of old ladies. Luckily, the ladies love Bialy. These bialys are similarly delicious and irresistible, but fair warning: You'll want to gargle some Listerine before meeting with your benefactors if you've eaten one of these oniony delights.

DOUGH

2 cups warm water, divided

One 2¼-teaspoon package active dry yeast

2 teaspoons sugar

2¼ teaspoons kosher salt

3½ cups all-purpose flour plus more for dusting

1¾ cups bread flour

TOPPING

1 tablespoon olive oil

⅓ cup minced onion

1½ teaspoons poppy seeds

½ teaspoon kosher salt

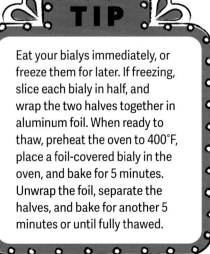

TIP

Eat your bialys immediately, or freeze them for later. If freezing, slice each bialy in half, and wrap the two halves together in aluminum foil. When ready to thaw, preheat the oven to 400°F, place a foil-covered bialy in the oven, and bake for 5 minutes. Unwrap the foil, separate the halves, and bake for another 5 minutes or until fully thawed.

YIELD: 8 BIALYS

1. To make the dough: Combine ½ cup warm water, the yeast, and the sugar in a large bowl. Let stand 10 minutes or until foamy.

2. Add the remaining 1½ cups warm water, salt, and both flours. Knead by hand or in a mixer with a dough hook for 8 minutes, until the dough is soft and smooth. (Too moist? Add a tablespoon of flour. Too dry? Add a tablespoon of water.)

3. Form dough into a ball, and place in an oiled bowl, rolling the dough in the bowl until all sides are oiled. Cover with plastic wrap, and let rise for 1½ to 2 hours or until the dough has doubled in size.

4. Place the dough on a floured cutting board. Cut into 8 equal pieces, and gently form each into a round about 1½ inches thick.

5. Move the rounds onto baking sheets covered in flour-dusted parchment paper. Cover with plastic wrap, and let rise for 1 hour.

6. While dough is rising, prepare the onion topping: Heat oil in a small sauté pan over medium heat and sauté onions until softened, about 3 minutes. In a small bowl, combine the cooked onions, poppy seeds, and kosher salt and set aside.

7. Preheat the oven to 425°F.

8. Make a wide, circular indentation in the middle of each dough round using your thumbs. (They should look like little pizzas with *a lot* of crust.)

9. Spread a heaping teaspoon of the onion mixture into each indentation.

10. Bake for 6 to 7 minutes, then turn the baking sheet around, and bake another 5 to 6 minutes. The bialys should be lightly browned but still soft.

11. Remove and cool on a wire rack.

Totally Shucked
Inspired By *Spring Awakening* (2006)

Yeah, you're shucked all right. You can kiss your sorry oysters goodbye. A bunch of hungry, hormonal adolescents came over and ate them all, and there's nothing left for you. That's the bitch of entertaining.

Next time, double this recipe, and you'll have plenty of tasty, cheesy broiled oysters on the half shell. Just make sure you clean them properly before shucking. Blah blah blah blah blah.

12 fresh oysters
Rock salt for baking
¼ cup shredded Emmentaler cheese
1 tablespoon bread crumbs
2 teaspoons chopped parsley
½ teaspoon kosher salt
½ teaspoon black pepper
½ teaspoon garlic powder
1 tablespoon salted butter

YIELD: 12 OYSTERS

1. Preheat your broiler with an oven rack 6 inches from the top.
2. Clean and shuck the oysters, leaving them in half shells.
3. Spread rock salt across a baking sheet, and balance the oyster shells on the rock salt.
4. Mix together the cheese, bread crumbs, parsley, salt, pepper, and garlic powder in a small bowl. Sprinkle the mixture evenly over the oysters.
5. Melt the butter in the microwave, and pour a small amount over each oyster.
6. Place the baking sheet on the top oven rack, and broil for 2 minutes or until cheese is melted and bread crumb mixture on top of the oysters is browned.

2

CHORUS TUNES

SIDES AND CONDIMENTS

• •

There are no small parts, only small plates.
While these side dishes may not get the
featured spot for dinner, they complement
the stars nicely and make the whole ensemble
really shine. Add one of these to a main dish
for a meal worthy of Best Dinner.

• •

Ol' Man River Rolls

Inspired By *Show Boat* (1927)

That old man Mississippi sure knows how to live. No matter what troubles come his way, he just keeps rolling along. These delicious cornbread-inspired rolls might give you a taste of what that's like, at least as long as your meal lasts. Pair them with catfish, fried chicken, or your favorite barbecue for a dinner fit for a Mississippi riverboat.

One 2¼-teaspoon package active dry yeast

¼ cup warm water

4 tablespoons honey, divided

1½ cups whole milk

2 teaspoons kosher salt

½ cup salted butter, cut into large chunks

½ cup cornmeal plus more for sprinkling

3 eggs, divided

3½ to 4 cups flour

1 tablespoon water

Honey butter for serving

YIELD: 24 ROLLS

1. Pour the yeast, warm water, and 2 tablespoons honey into the bowl of your stand mixer, and stir to combine. Let sit for 10 minutes or until foamy.

2. Place milk, salt, and butter in a medium sauce pot and bring to a simmer over medium heat. Slowly stir in the cornmeal and cook, stirring often, for 2 minutes or until the mixture has thickened. Set aside to cool.

3. Add the cooled cornmeal mixture, the remaining 2 tablespoons honey, and 2 eggs to the yeast mixture. Add flour, ½ cup at a time, while slowly mixing with the dough hook attachment. If the dough has too much liquid, add another ½ cup of flour. Knead with the dough hook for 5 minutes.

4. Move the dough to a large oiled bowl, roll the dough once so it's fully oiled, and cover the bowl with plastic wrap. Let rise for 1 to 2 hours or until the dough has doubled in size.

5. Cover two baking sheets with parchment paper and sprinkle cornmeal on top. Set aside.

6. Punch down the risen dough, and place it on a lightly floured surface. Cut it into 24 equal pieces. Roll each section into a ball and place on the baking sheets. Cover with plastic wrap, and let rise for another 30 minutes.

7. Preheat the oven to 375°F. Beat 1 egg with 1 tablespoon of water to make the egg wash, and brush the top of each roll. Sprinkle the rolls with some additional cornmeal.

8. Bake the rolls for 15 to 20 minutes or until golden brown. Let cool for 5 minutes, then serve with honey butter.

Too Darn Hot Sauce
Inspired by *Kiss Me, Kate* (1948)

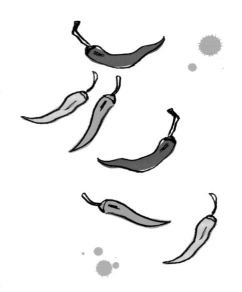

Quick question for the company of *Kiss Me, Kate*: If it's too darn hot to meet up with your baby, is a high-speed, six-minute tap number in the middle of your show really going to help? Don't think too darn hard about it. Save some energy to make this sauce instead. It's guaranteed to make any dish just hot enough.

5 poblano peppers
5 serrano peppers
3 jalapeño peppers
2 habanero peppers
2 tablespoons vegetable oil
4 cloves garlic, minced
1 cup white vinegar
½ tablespoon kosher salt

YIELD: ONE 12-TO-16-OUNCE BOTTLE OF SAUCE

1. Cut the tops off the peppers and cut the peppers into thick slices.
2. Place the oil, garlic, and peppers in a large pot. Sauté for 2 minutes, or until peppers have softened, and then add the vinegar and salt.
3. Cover the pot, bring the mixture to a boil, and then reduce heat to a simmer for 10 minutes.
4. Remove the pot from the heat, and let cool slightly. (Use caution when removing the lid from the pot—the steam that comes out will burn your eyes!)
5. Pour the mixture into a blender, and blend until liquified.
6. Strain through a fine-mesh sieve, and store the liquid in a 16-ounce bottle or mason jar. It should last a couple months in the fridge.

TIP

Be careful working with this recipe! Use gloves while cutting and handling the peppers, and keep the area ventilated while cooking (open windows and turn the stove fan on). If the sauce is just too darn hot for you as written, remove the habaneros and scrape some of the seeds out of the peppers before sautéing them.

Professor Harold Dill

Inspired by *The Music Man* (1957)

Friends, this recipe is no Trouble at all. I said no Trouble with a capital *T* and that rhymes with *D* and that stands for *dill.* Just as Professor Harold Hill created something special out of the boys in River City, you can do the same with some cucumbers and a bit of time. After a couple days, the crunch of these tangy pickles will be as sweet to your ears as the sound of seventy-six trombones on parade.

¾ pound Kirby or Persian cucumbers (4 to 5 cucumbers)

Ice water

7 sprigs fresh dill

1 teaspoon black peppercorns

4 cloves garlic

1 teaspoon dill seeds

½ teaspoon coriander seeds

½ cup distilled white vinegar

½ cup water

1 tablespoon kosher or pickling salt

1 teaspoon sugar

YIELD: 5 FULL PICKLES OR 20 PICKLE SPEARS

1. Cut the tips off the cucumbers, and submerge in a bowl full of ice water. Cover and refrigerate for 4 to 5 hours. (This will help the pickles stay nice and crunchy while soaking.)
2. Place the dill, peppercorns, garlic, and coriander and dill seeds in a wide-mouth pint jar. Put the cucumbers in the jar. (Keep them whole or cut them into spears if you prefer.)
3. Bring the vinegar, water, salt, and sugar to a boil in a small saucepan, and boil for one minute or until the salt and sugar are fully dissolved.
4. Pour the hot brine into the jar and seal. Let cool to room temperature, and then refrigerate.
5. Keep sealed in the fridge for at least two days, and then taste your pickles. They'll keep in the fridge for up to a month—but we doubt they'll last that long.

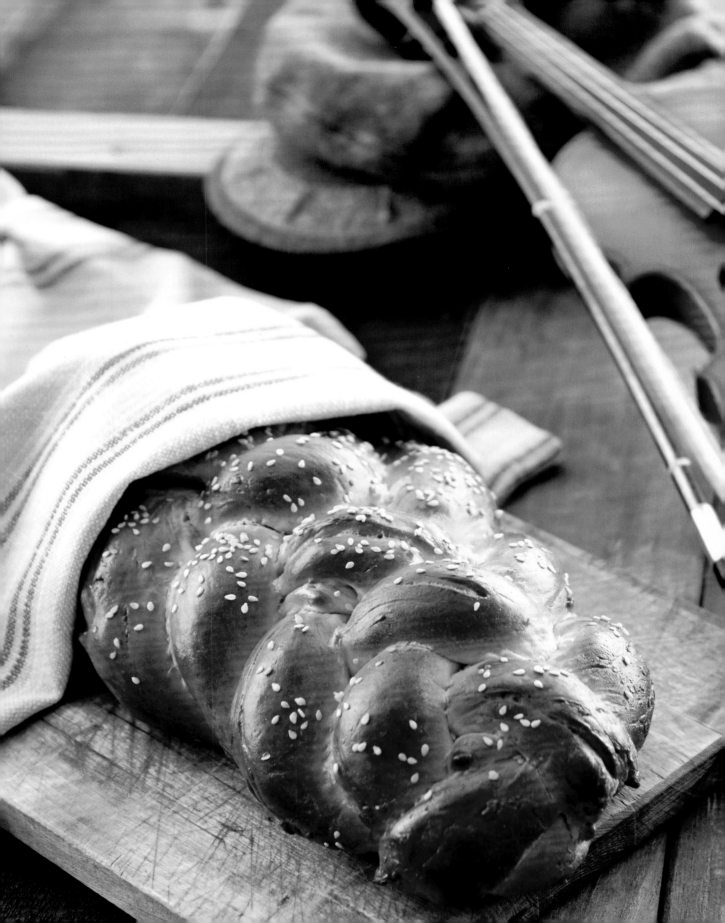

Tradition-al Challah

Inspired by *Fiddler on the Roof* (1964)

Ah, tradition. It's a beautiful thing—when challah is involved. This delicious, slightly sweet bread is often saved for Shabbat and other special occasions, but you can make it any time. Just be sure to follow the instructions carefully. Making challah can be as tricky and touchy as a fiddler on the roof, but tradition will help you keep your balance and make your family proud. Make it well enough and Yente may even be able to find you a match!

One 2¼-teaspoon packet active dry yeast
1 teaspoon sugar
½ cup warm water
3 eggs, divided
⅓ cup honey
¼ cup vegetable oil
1½ teaspoons kosher salt
4½ cups bread flour
1 tablespoon water
Sesame seeds for topping (optional)

YIELD: 1 LOAF

1. Mix the yeast, sugar, and ½ cup of warm water in a large mixing bowl. Let sit for 10 minutes, until the yeast has started to look foamy.
2. Add 2 eggs, honey, oil, and salt. Whisk together.
3. Add the flour ½ cup at a time, mixing between each addition with a spatula. When you can no longer easily mix it, use your hands to knead the dough after each addition. If the dough is sticking to your hands after 4½ cups of flour, add another ½ cup.
4. Cover the bowl with plastic wrap, and place it in a warm place to rise—around 1½ to 2 hours depending on temperature. It may not double in size, but it should be significantly puffy.
5. Punch down the dough, and let rest on a lightly floured surface for 10 minutes.

Continued on page 38

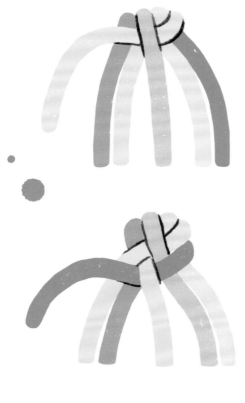

6. Braid the dough: Separate into 6 equal parts, and roll each out flat. Roll each flat piece into a rope about 16 inches long, slightly tapered at each end. Line them all up, and pinch the tops together. Lift the rightmost rope over the next two, under the next, and then over the final two. It should now be the leftmost rope. Repeat the braid with the new rightmost rope. Continue until you reach the ends of the ropes. Crimp the bottom ends together like you did with the tops.
7. Place the braided dough on a parchment paper–lined cookie sheet to rise for another hour. While the dough is rising, preheat the oven to 350°F.
8. Mix 1 egg and 1 tablespoon of water. Brush the egg wash on top of the bread. Sprinkle sesame seeds on top.
9. Bake the challah for 20 minutes, and then turn the pan around and bake for another 20 minutes.
10. Remove the challah from the oven and turn over. Tap on the bottom of the loaf. Does it sound hollow? That means it's done. Turn back over and let cool on a cooling rack.

TIP

While challah is great on its own, you can dress it up a bit by adding 1½ cups of raisins or chocolate chips to the dough after you add all of the flour.

A Sunny Ball of Butter

Inspired by *Funny Girl* (1964)

Sometimes our friends think they have our best interest at heart. "Don't run off and marry that man," they say. "Don't give up your flourishing career." "Don't have a giant ball of butter for breakfast." Well, who are they to tell you what to do? Don't let them rain on your parade—life's juicy and you've gotta have your bite.

   This sunny ball of butter will start your morning off right. You'll want to put this bright, orange-flavored butter on all your breakfast food: scones, toast, pancakes, waffles, muffins, and more.

1 small orange
1 cup salted butter
¼ cup honey

YIELD: 1 CUP

1. Cut the orange in half. Take one half and zest 2 teaspoons.
2. Whip butter in a mixer or food processor until light and fluffy.
3. Add the honey and orange zest to the butter and mix.
4. Place the butter onto a sheet of waxed paper, and using the waxed paper, shape the butter into a sphere.
5. Wrap completely in plastic wrap, and refrigerate until firm (about an hour).
6. Slice thin wedges from the other half of the orange, and decorate the butter sphere with the slices by sticking them in around the butter to represent the sun's rays. Serve with a small butter or cheese knife.

I'm Still Schmear

Inspired by *Follies* (1971)

Follies is all about nostalgia, and while Carlotta dwells on the past, she reminds us that even after all the ups and downs of her career, she's still here. Ask any former New Yorker about bagels and schmear, and they might launch into a similar soliloquy. Remind them that they're still schmear with this whipped everything-bagel cream cheese.

½ tablespoon poppy seeds

¼ tablespoon white sesame seeds

¼ tablespoon black sesame seeds (or substitute additional white sesame seeds)

¼ tablespoon dried garlic flakes

¼ tablespoon dried onion flakes

½ teaspoon sea salt flakes

8 ounces cream cheese

2 tablespoons whole milk

1 bagel, toasted

Lox, red onion slices, and capers for topping (optional)

YIELD: 10 OUNCES

1. Mix together the poppy seeds, sesame seeds, garlic, onion, and salt. Set aside.
2. Whip the cream cheese in a mixer on high for 2 minutes. Add the milk, and whip together until light and fluffy.
3. Add the everything-bagel seasoning to the cream cheese, and mix until fully incorporated.
4. To serve, spread on a freshly toasted bagel. Top with lox, red onion, and capers.
5. Lament about how New York and Broadway just aren't what they used to be.

I Yam What I Yam

Inspired by *La Cage aux Folles* (1983)

You are what you are. You're not just a simple baked yam. You're something a little fancy, a little fabulous, but still grounded and good for those who love you. You are a duchess yam, and you want everyone to know it. So open up your closet (*ahem*, kitchen), and share your sparkle with the world.

2 pounds yams (about 4 medium yams), peeled and roughly chopped

¼ cup butter

3 eggs, divided

½ teaspoon kosher salt

¼ teaspoon ground nutmeg

¼ teaspoon black pepper

1 tablespoon maple syrup

1 teaspoon heavy whipping cream

YIELD: 18 YAM ROSETTES

1. Preheat oven to 400°F, and line a baking sheet with parchment paper.
2. Fill a large pot with at least 4 inches water. Add the yams, and bring to a boil. Reduce to a simmer, and let cook 20 minutes, until the yams are fully soft.
3. Drain the pot, and let the potatoes release steam for a couple minutes.
4. Add the butter to the pot, and mash the potatoes. Separate two of the eggs and discard the whites. Add the egg yolks, salt, nutmeg, pepper, and maple syrup, and mix until smooth.
5. Transfer the potato mixture to a pastry bag with a star tip. Pipe the mixture onto the baking sheet in 2-inch rosettes.
6. Whisk the remaining egg and heavy cream together, and brush onto the tops of the rosettes.
7. Bake for 20 minutes or until golden brown.
8. Serve on your finest "Greek leapfrog" dishes.

The Internet Is for Corn
Inspired by *Avenue Q* (2003)

Puppets are a great tool for teaching children life lessons: how to play with others, how to be a good neighbor, how to tell right from wrong. Thanks to *Avenue Q*, we know puppets can teach adults some equally important life lessons: It sucks to be us, everyone's a little bit racist, and the internet is for porn. Remember that lesson fondly as you eat this phallic roasted corn with creamy, spicy topping. Too far? It's never far enough for these little felt monsters.

4 ears of corn
1 teaspoon kosher salt
½ teaspoon chili powder
½ teaspoon paprika
½ teaspoon ground cumin
½ teaspoon black pepper
½ cup mayonnaise
¼ cup crumbled cotija or grated Parmesan cheese
1 lime, quartered, for serving

YIELD: 4 EARS OF CORN

1. Preheat a grill to medium-high.
2. Shuck the corn: Strip the husks down to the base of the corn, and snap off the bottom nobs. Remove any stray silks.
3. Turning often, grill corn for 10 to 15 minutes or until tender and charred all over.
4. Mix together the salt, chili powder, paprika, cumin, and black pepper. Set aside.
5. Spread the mayonnaise over the corn, and then sprinkle the spice mixture evenly over the mayo. Sprinkle the cheese on top. Serve with lime wedges.

TIP

Not into mayo? Cover the corn in salted butter instead!

Pain du 24601

Inspired by *Les Misérables* (1986)

The loaf of bread Jean Valjean steals is not the typical French baguette. It's *larton brutal*, or "black bread," a dark, dense rye bread that commoners were more likely to eat. This recipe makes a lighter—yet still dense and chewy—modern version of the bread, much tastier than the loaf Jean Valjean would've stolen to survive in eighteenth-century France. It might not be worth 19 years in prison, but top a warm slice with some butter, and it's anything but miserable.

One 2¼-teaspoon packet active dry yeast
¾ cup warm water
3 tablespoons dark brown sugar
1½ cups water to boil
½ teaspoon kosher salt
1 cup cornmeal plus more for dusting
1⅔ cup bread flour plus more for dusting
1 cup rye flour
½ tsp baking powder

YIELD: 2 LOAVES OF BREAD

1. Combine the yeast, ¼ cup warm water, and brown sugar in the bowl of your stand mixer. Let stand for 10 minutes or until the yeast is foamy.
2. In a small saucepan, stir the salt into 1½ cups water, and bring to a boil. Add in the cornmeal, and cook, stirring often, about 2 minutes. Set aside to cool.
3. Sift together the flours and baking powder in a separate bowl. Set aside.
4. Add the cooled cornmeal mixture to the yeast mixture in the bowl of your stand mixer and mix on low until combined. Then slowly add in the flour mixture while continuing to mix. Once combined, knead with the dough hook attachment or with your hands on a floured surface for 3 minutes or until it makes a fully formed and springy dough. Cover dough in the bowl with plastic wrap and let rise for 1 hour or until doubled in size.
5. Remove the dough from the bowl, and place on a floured surface. Split the dough in half, shape each half into an oblong loaf, and place on a cornmeal-covered baking sheet. Cover with plastic wrap, and let rise for 1 more hour.
6. Place a tray of water on the bottom rack of a cold oven, and then preheat the oven to 400°F. (The water will help steam the bread and create a fantastic crust as it cooks.)
7. Bake for 40 minutes or until the loaves sound hollow when you tap the bottoms. Remove from the oven, and let cool on a wire rack.

Lady Marmalade

Inspired by *Moulin Rouge!* (2019)

The ladies of the Moulin Rouge are a little sweet and a little spicy—and depending on how you tip, they might be a bit bitter. You won't easily forget your time with them, as you won't forget this sweet and spiced marmalade. It'll leave you asking for more, more, more!

4 oranges
2 cups sugar
½ cup water
2 tablespoons lemon juice
1 teaspoon vanilla
1 cinnamon stick
1 whole star anise
4 whole cloves

YIELD: 12 TO 16 OUNCES

1. Using a vegetable peeler, peel the zest from the oranges, avoiding the white pith. Carefully cut away any pith attached to the zest. Set the zest aside.
2. Using a small, sharp knife, cut the pith from the orange and discard.
3. Julienne the zest, and dice the oranges. Place zest and oranges in a medium saucepan with the sugar, water, lemon juice, vanilla, cinnamon stick, star anise, and cloves.
4. Bring the mixture to a boil, and then reduce heat and simmer uncovered, stirring occasionally, until a thermometer reaches 220°F (around 1 hour).
5. To test that your marmalade has set, place a small amount on a chilled plate, and run your finger through it. If the marmalade stays put and doesn't run back into the valley, it's set.
6. Transfer the marmalade to a mason jar and seal. Store in the refrigerator for up to three months.

3

SHOWSTOPPERS

ENTRÉES

• •

And now, for the moment you've been waiting
for: the big number, the star attraction, the
main dish. These crowd-pleasing entrees are
the culinary equivalent of the moment your
favorite Broadway star takes center stage to
belt out their signature number. Learn them,
love them, savor them. And if you make one
of these masterpieces for guests, demand
a standing ovation. After all, they're in the
presence of greatness.

• •

Schnitzel With Noodles

Inspired by *The Sound of Music* (1959)

Thunder and lightning got you feeling sad? Take some advice from Maria, and find comfort in some of your favorite things. Comfort food, that is.

While egg noodles are great with schnitzel, we're going authentically Austrian and making spaetzle: tiny German dumplings made from a simple mixture of eggs, milk, and flour. And then we're making it even more amazing by adding everyone's actual favorite thing: cheese. It only takes a bit more work, and the chewy pasta makes for a delicious pairing with the pork cutlets. You'll be ready to say *auf wiedersehen* to your bad mood before you know it.

SPAETZLE

1 cup all-purpose flour
½ teaspoon kosher salt
¼ teaspoon black pepper
½ teaspoon ground nutmeg
2 eggs
¼ cup whole milk plus 2 tablespoons
1 tablespoon butter
¾ cup Emmentaler cheese
1 tablespoon diced chives

SCHNITZEL

4 boneless pork cutlets
¼ teaspoon paprika
¼ teaspoon garlic powder
Salt and pepper, to taste
½ cup whole milk
2 eggs
½ cup flour
1 cup bread crumbs
¼ cup vegetable oil
1 lemon, quartered

YIELD: 4 SERVINGS

1. To make the spaetzle: Combine flour, salt, pepper, and nutmeg in a bowl. Mix in the eggs and ¼ cup milk until a nice dough forms. Set the dough aside to rest.
2. Bring a medium pot of salted water to boil.
3. In the meantime, start the schnitzel: Using a meat mallet or tenderizer, pound the pork cutlets to ¼-inch thickness. Mix together the paprika, garlic powder, salt, and pepper, and season both sides of each cutlet with the spice mixture. Whisk together the milk and eggs in a shallow bowl and set aside. Place the flour on a large plate or in a shallow bowl and the bread crumbs in another.
4. Heat the oil in a large pan on medium-high. One at a time, coat the pork cutlets in the flour, then the egg-milk mixture, and then the bread crumbs. Without crowding the pan, cook the cutlets in batches for 4 minutes on each side until golden brown and crispy. Move the finished cutlets to a paper towel–lined plate.
5. To finish the spaetzle: When your pot of water reaches a boil, oil a spaetzle maker or potato ricer, and press the dough through it into the boiling water. (You can also use a colander or grater with large holes. Place the spaetzle dough inside the colander or grater, and press it through with a spatula, letting it drop into the water.) Let the dumplings cook until they start floating on the surface of the water, about 2 minutes. Rinse the spaetzle with cold water and drain.
6. Toss the noodles in a medium pan on medium-high heat with the butter until slightly browned, about 5 minutes. Add the cheese, chives, and 2 tablespoons of milk, and cook until cheese has fully melted into a thick sauce, stirring often.
7. Divide the spaetzle between four plates, and serve with a schnitzel cutlet and a lemon wedge.

Gruel, Glorious Gruel
Inspired by *Oliver!* (1962)

The poor orphan boys of *Oliver!* get nothing but gruel every day while dreaming of real, wonderful, marvelous, glorious food. Look, gruel is not good. Think of a bowl of milk, boiled for hours with a couple tablespoons of oats. Maybe some salt. So, in Oliver's honor, we're making a version he and the boys wouldn't have tired of—a thick, flavorful oatmeal topped with piles of peaches, cream, and other goodies.

2 cups whole milk

2 cups water

2 cups old-fashioned rolled oats

½ cup kosher salt

1½ teaspoons cinnamon, divided

1 tablespoon unsalted butter

2 peaches, peeled and sliced thin (about ¼-inch thick)

2 tablespoons brown sugar plus more for serving

½ cup heavy whipping cream

1 cup pecans

Honey for serving

YIELD: 4 SERVINGS

1. Bring the milk and water to a boil in a medium saucepan. Add the oats, salt, and 1 teaspoon cinnamon, and stir. Simmer for 10 minutes or until the oats are your preferred texture. (For creamier oats, simmer for another 5 to 10 minutes.)

2. While the oats are simmering, melt the butter in a medium pan. Add the peaches, the brown sugar, and the other ½ teaspoon cinnamon. Sauté for 5 minutes, stirring occasionally.

3. Divide the oats into four bowls. Top with equal portions of peaches, cream, and pecans. Serve with a drizzle of honey and a sprinkle of brown sugar.

Turkey and Dumplings
Inspired by *Hello, Dolly!* (1964)

Dolly is good at many things, but perhaps her most impressive skill is eating an entire banquet by herself while ignoring the chaos around her. Replicate her meal and enjoy—but try not to eat it quite as fast as she does. While these potato dumplings will melt in your mouth, they don't melt as quickly as the cotton candy or edible paper concoctions they use on stage.

TURKEY LEGS

1 tablespoon paprika

1 tablespoon garlic powder

1 teaspoon dried thyme

1 teaspoon dried rosemary

1 teaspoon kosher salt

½ teaspoon black pepper

4 turkey legs

¼ cup softened butter

POTATO DUMPLINGS

10 medium potatoes (about 3 pounds), peeled and quartered

1 cup flour

2 eggs

1 tablespoon dried chives

1 tablespoon garlic powder

2 teaspoons kosher salt

2 tablespoons butter

2 tablespoons oil

TIP

Pair this meal with some beets and your favorite gravy—great for dipping the turkey in, drinking, and using as impromptu perfume.

YIELD: 4 SERVINGS (OR 1 DOLLY-SIZED SERVING)

1. To make the turkey legs: Preheat the oven to 400°F.
2. Combine the paprika, garlic powder, thyme, rosemary, salt, and pepper, and set aside.
3. Cover the turkey legs in butter, and then rub the spice mixture all over the legs, both inside and outside the skin.
4. Place the turkey legs on a roasting rack or in a roasting pan covered in foil, and roast for 1 hour. Turn the legs over, reduce the temperature to 350°F, and roast for 30 more minutes or until juices coming out of the turkey run clear.
5. To make the potato dumplings: While the turkey is cooking, place the potatoes in a Dutch oven or large, heavy pot. Fill with water until the potatoes are covered, and bring to a boil. Reduce heat and cook 15 minutes or until tender. Drain.
6. Mash the potatoes in the pot, and let cool for 5 minutes. Add the flour, eggs, chives, garlic powder, and salt. Mix.
7. Shape 20 golf ball–sized balls, and put aside on a plate.
8. Rinse out the Dutch oven, and fill it with water. Bring the water to a boil, and add the potato balls. Simmer for 7 to 9 minutes or until a toothpick inserted in the dumplings comes out clean.
9. Heat the butter and oil in a large skillet on medium-high heat, and sauté the dumplings until they begin to brown, about 5 minutes.
10. Take the turkey out of the oven, let rest for 10 minutes, and serve with the dumplings.

Age of Asparagus
Inspired by *Hair* (1968)

This is the dawning of the age of asparagus. A time to eat vegetables grown from this great earth, dodge the draft, and stock up on hallucinogens. Well, that escalated quickly. Let's start with the veggies and see where the day takes us, OK? This vegan recipe incorporates asparagus, angel *hair* pasta, and sunshiny lemon for a delicious and nourishing dish that won't harm any of Mother Earth's creatures. Far out.

8 ounces angel hair pasta
2 tablespoons pine nuts
1½ pounds asparagus
2 tablespoons olive oil
4 cloves garlic, halved
Salt and pepper, to taste
¼ cup vegetable broth
Juice of 1 lemon (about 2 tablespoons)
Red pepper flakes, to taste

YIELD: 4 SERVINGS

1. Boil a large pot of salted water. Add the angel hair pasta, and cook according to package directions. Drain the pasta, reserving ¼ cup of the pasta water.
2. In a dry large-sized pan, roast pine nuts on medium heat, stirring often, until lightly browned (about 90 seconds). Remove from pan and set aside.
3. Trim off the tough bottoms of the asparagus, and cut the rest into 1-inch pieces.
4. Heat olive oil in the pan you used for the pine nuts. Add the asparagus, garlic, salt, and pepper, and sauté over medium-high heat until the asparagus is tender, about 5 minutes. Add vegetable broth and pasta water, and heat until warmed, about 2 minutes.
5. Place the angel hair in a large bowl, and pour the broth and vegetable mixture on top. Add the lemon juice, roasted pine nuts, and red pepper flakes to taste. Mix.
6. Add forks to the large bowl, and eat together family style on a blanket at a be-in.

TIP

Not entirely "one with the earth," and don't mind a bit of cheese? Top your pasta with some grated parmesan. I won't tell the commune if you don't.

Mama's Well-Peppered Ragù

Inspired by *Chicago* (1975)

Whether you're guilty of murder or not, there are two things you want to do when you get to prison: Appeal to the sensibilities of Billy Flynn, and get on Mama Morton's good side. Offer to work in the cafeteria, and pepper her ragù extra well. You'll go far. This dish is full of spice, includes bell pepper, black pepper, *and* red pepper flakes, and it makes a big enough pot to feed all of Murderess Row. So put on your best black fishnets; it's time to get cookin', honey.

1 tablespoon olive oil plus ¼ cup

1 carrot, minced

1 yellow onion, minced

1 red bell pepper, diced

1 stalk celery, minced

4 cloves garlic, minced

1 pound ground beef

¼ pound ground spicy Italian sausage

24 ounces crushed tomatoes

6 ounces tomato paste

½ cup red wine

1 bay leaf

1 tablespoon dried oregano

2 tablespoons dried basil

½ to 1 teaspoon red pepper flakes (adjust to spice preference)

1 teaspoon black pepper plus more to taste

Salt, to taste

1 pound tagliatelle

YIELD: 8 SERVINGS

1. In a large pot or Dutch oven, heat 1 tablespoon olive oil over medium-high heat, and sauté the carrot, onion, red pepper, celery, and garlic for 2 to 3 minutes or until softened. Add the ground meat and cook until browned, stirring occasionally so the ingredients are evenly cooked.
2. Add tomatoes, tomato paste, ¼ cup olive oil, wine, bay leaf, oregano, basil, red pepper flakes, and black pepper. Bring everything to a boil, then reduce heat to a bubbling simmer. Cook uncovered at this heat for at least 2 hours, stirring occasionally. Salt and pepper to taste.
3. Boil a large pot of salty water, and cook tagliatelle according to package instructions. Drain the tagliatelle (don't rinse), reserving ½ cup of the pasta water.
4. Add the pasta water to the sauce and mix.
5. Mix the sauce into a large bowl of the pasta and serve family style.

Frank-N-Furter's Meat Loaf

Inspired by *The Rocky Horror Show* (1975)

Hot patootie, this is one tasty meat loaf. Just the thing Frank might make for his party guests after a long day in the lab creating his next masterpiece. We recommend beef, but whatever ground meat you fancy will do. Whatever you use, don't get it too lean—this isn't a Rocky Loaf, after all. This sexy 1970s-style loaf will make you want to do a time warp and eat it all over again.

MEAT LOAF

2 pounds ground beef

2 cups bread crumbs

1 cup whole milk

2 eggs, slightly beaten

1 cup minced yellow onion

6 cloves garlic, minced

4 tablespoons ketchup

2 tablespoons Worcestershire sauce

1 tablespoon kosher salt

2 teaspoons black pepper

GLAZE

1 cup ketchup

¼ cup brown sugar

2 tablespoons Worcestershire sauce

YIELD: 8 SERVINGS

1. Preheat oven to 350°F. Line a loaf pan with parchment paper, letting a little excess hang over the edge.
2. To make the meat loaf: Mix all meat loaf ingredients together in a large bowl, being careful not to overmix. Spoon the mixture in the loaf pan and spread evenly to all sides.
3. To make the glaze: Mix together the ketchup and brown sugar, and glaze the top of the meat loaf with half of the mixture.
4. Bake for 1 hour. Lift the parchment paper by the edges to cleanly remove the meat loaf from the pan and place on a serving plate.
5. Glaze with the second half of the ketchup mixture. Let rest for 10 minutes.
6. Cut into thick slices and serve with some hot patooties—whoops—potatoes.

The Wurst Pies in London

Inspired by *Sweeney Todd: The Demon Barber of Fleet Street* (1979)

Mrs. Lovett's pies are filled with lard and, well, we all know what else. Obviously we're going in a slightly different direction. With a little bit of bratwurst, we can turn the worst pies in London into the *wurst* pies—cozy British-inspired pies that'll knock the socks off Mrs. Mooney's. A little bit of ale cooked into the pie adds an extra layer of flavor, and no one will discourage you from having a pint on the side as well. Best of all: No cats or priests are harmed in the making of this recipe. Times aren't that hard.

PIE CRUST

3 cups flour plus more for dusting
1 teaspoon kosher salt
1 cup cold unsalted butter
½ cup cold water

FILLING

2 tablespoons oil
1 pound bratwursts, sliced ½ inch thick
1 cup diced red potatoes
1 medium yellow onion, diced
2 carrots, diced
2 cloves garlic, minced
1 teaspoon dried thyme
1 teaspoon dried rosemary
1 teaspoon kosher salt
½ teaspoon pepper
1 tablespoon flour
1 cup ale
¼ cup heavy whipping cream

EGG WASH

1 egg
1 tablespoon water

YIELD: 6 PIES

1. To make the pie crust: Mix together the flour and salt in a large bowl. Then cut in the butter using a pastry blender or your hands. Add the cold water, and mix it in with your hands until a dough forms.

2. Remove the dough from the bowl, and press into a disc. Wrap in plastic wrap, and refrigerate until the filling is made, at least 15 minutes.

3. To make the filling: Sauté the bratwursts, potatoes, onion, carrots, and garlic in a large sauté pan or skillet over medium-high heat. Cook for 5 minutes or until brats are fully cooked and vegetables are softened. Add the thyme, rosemary, salt, pepper, and flour. Stir to combine, then add the ale and cream. Simmer for 5 minutes or until the liquid has thickened.

4. Preheat the oven to 400°F.

5. To finish the dough: Remove from the fridge and cut into six equal pieces. Place on a floured surface, and roll four pieces into 8-inch circles. Take the other two pieces, and cut them each in half. Roll them out into four 5-inch circles.

6. Place the 8-inch circles in four-inch pie pans, pressing the dough into the edges and letting the excess stick out the top.

7. Fill each pie cavity with the meat filling (around ½ to ¾ cup in each), and then top with the 5-inch circles, crimping the edges together. Poke two holes in the top middle of each pie.

8. To make the egg wash: Whisk together the egg and 1 tablespoon water, and brush the egg wash over each crust.

9. Bake for 25 minutes or until golden brown. Let cool for at least 5 minutes before serving.

Pasta With Meatless Balls

Inspired by *Rent* (1996)

The Life Café: rendezvous for local artists and hot spot for all that trendy '90s vegetarian cuisine. While the café itself no longer exists, we can pay homage to the spot where Jonathan Larson wrote most of *Rent* by making an item inspired by their menu. Are you normally a meat eater? Get off your Range Rover and live *la vie bohème* for a bit. Feeding a large group? Serve with thirteen orders of fries and plenty of wine and beer.

2 tablespoons olive oil plus more for frying

½ cup diced yellow onion

1½ cups diced mushrooms

4 cloves garlic, minced

1 cup oats

½ cup bread crumbs

¼ cup shredded Parmesan cheese or vegan Parmesan cheese

2 teaspoons dried basil

2 teaspoons dried parsley

1 teaspoon dried oregano

1 teaspoon dried rosemary

One 15½ ounce can of garbanzo beans, drained but not rinsed

1 tablespoon tomato paste

Salt and black pepper, to taste

1 egg (or substitute flaxseed egg)

1 jar marinara sauce (around 24 ounces)

1 package of your favorite pasta

YIELD: 24 MEATLESS BALLS OR 8 SERVINGS WITH PASTA

1. Heat 2 tablespoons olive oil in a large sauté pan on medium heat, and add the onion. Cook for 2 minutes or until the onions become translucent.
2. Add the mushrooms and garlic, and cook for another 3 minutes. Take the pan off the heat, and let cool for a few minutes.
3. In a small bowl, combine the oats, bread crumbs, Parmesan cheese, basil, parsley, oregano, and rosemary. Pour into a food processor or blender, and pulse until contents are mixed and oats are minced but not powdery. Place back into the small bowl and set aside.
4. Add the sautéed veggies, garbanzo beans, and tomato paste to a food processor or blender. Pulse until everything is just combined, but not liquified.
5. Transfer the contents of the blender to a large bowl. Add the dry ingredients, and mix until everything is thoroughly combined.
6. Taste the mixture. Add salt and pepper to taste, if needed. Add the egg and mix.
7. Form the meatless balls into golf ball–sized balls with a cookie scoop or your hands.
8. Pour marinara sauce into a medium saucepot, and bring to a simmer.
9. Fill the bottom of the large pan with olive oil, and set to medium-high heat. Fry the meatballs until golden brown, about 2 minutes per side.
10. Place the fried meatballs in the saucepot, and let simmer in the sauce for 10 minutes.
11. While the meatballs are simmering, cook your favorite pasta per package directions. I recommend a hearty whole-grain spaghetti.
12. Serve the meatballs and sauce over a generous helping of pasta. Don't forget the wine and beer!

The King's Pastrami on Rye
Inspired by *Newsies* (2012)

Like many New Yorkers, when the newsies dream of being King of New York, some of their first thoughts are about getting a giant pastrami sandwich. This sandwich is the authentic New York Jewish deli pastrami on rye, but with a practical twist. Take the pickle that's normally served on the side, slice it, and add it to the sandwich. You're a Newsie—you've got to keep a hand free to sell those papes. Now go out there and seize the day!

¾ pound sliced pastrami
2 thick slices rye bread
Spicy brown mustard for spreading
1 large deli-style sour pickle

YIELD: 1 SANDWICH

1. Warm up the pastrami by steaming it: Place an inch of water in a large pot and a steamer basket on top. Cover and let steam for 10 minutes or until pastrami is fully warmed.
2. Toast the rye bread, and thickly slather one side of each slice with mustard.
3. Carefully stack all the pastrami on one slice of bread.
4. Slice the pickle lengthwise to create long, thick slices. Place the slices on top of your mountain of meat.
5. Top the sandwich with the other piece of bread, and slice in half. Eat like a king!

Newfoundland Toutons

Inspired by *Come From Away* (2017)

The residents of Gander, Newfoundland are known for being extremely hospitable, and that hospitality was never more appreciated than on September 11, 2001, when seven thousand "come from aways" ended up stranded in their small town. The best way to comfort these folks? With some warm, cozy, traditional food, of course. Newfoundland toutons (*tout* rhymes with *pout*) are what pancakes wish they could be. Perfect this recipe, and you too could become an honorary Newfoundlander. We won't even make you kiss the cod.

1½ teaspoons active dry yeast

½ cup warm water

3½ cups flour

1 tablespoon sugar

1 teaspoon kosher salt

1½ tablespoons salted butter, melted, plus more for topping

1 cup warm whole milk

4 slices thick-cut bacon

Molasses or maple syrup for topping

TIP

Toutons are traditionally made with grease from salt pork back fat. We're using bacon grease because it's a bit easier to find, but feel free to go the traditional route if you have the means. The beauty of this recipe is that it can be made with leftover white bread dough or pizza dough. If you have either of those lying around, skip ahead to step 6.

YIELD: 18 TOUTONS (ABOUT 6 SERVINGS)

1. Dissolve the yeast into the warm water. Let sit for 10 minutes or until foamy.
2. Mix the flour, sugar, and salt together in a large stand mixer.
3. Add the melted butter, milk, and yeast mixture to the flour. Mix with a dough hook starting on low and increasing to medium speed for 9 to 10 minutes.
4. Cover the bowl, and let the dough rise for 1 hour or until nearly doubled in size.
5. Punch down the dough, and let rest for another 10 minutes.
6. Cook the bacon in a large sauté pan or skillet over medium heat. Set bacon on a paper towel–covered plate to cool. Leave the bacon grease in the pan, and raise the temperature on the burner to medium-high.
7. Cut off sections of the dough about the size of a golf ball, and flatten them in your palms to make ½-inch-thick discs.
8. Fry the dough in the bacon-greased pan for about 3 minutes each side or until golden brown.
9. Top each touton with a square of butter and a drizzle of molasses, maple syrup, or topping of your choice. Serve with the bacon on the side.

4

ELEVEN O'CLOCK NUMBER

COCKTAILS

• •

It's getting late—time for one more heart-tugging, soul-stirring number before you go. Fair warning, effects of the eleven o'clock number can vary from person to person: You may end up singing and dancing in the street, or you may end up sitting alone in the dark facing some hard truths about your life. Either way, we promise it'll go down real well. Sit down, drink up, and enjoy the final scenes of the night.

• •

Old-Fashioned Wedding

Inspired by *Annie Get Your Gun* (1946)

Like many couples, Frank and Annie have different ideas about what kind of wedding they should have. But even the most hardheaded of partners—or the most bitter of rivals—should be able to agree that this sweet drink is a winner. This *Annie Get Your Gun*–inspired cocktail is a wedding-themed version of an old-fashioned, with notes of cake and orange blossoms. But don't worry—there's still enough bourbon to make Annie happy.

¼ ounce simple syrup
2 dashes orange bitters
1 teaspoon orange flower water
½ ounce hazelnut liqueur
1 large ice cube
2 ounces bourbon
Orange twist for garnishing

YIELD: 1 COCKTAIL

1. Add simple syrup, bitters, orange flower water, and hazelnut liqueur to an old-fashioned glass. Stir to combine.
2. Add a large ice cube, and pour the bourbon over the top. Give it a quick stir, and garnish with an orange twist.

Another Vodka Stinger

Inspired by *Company* (1970)

Here's to the ladies who lunch. And to the ladies who openly judge them after a few drinks. This recipe makes a vodka stinger with a second drink on deck in ice cube form, so you never need to request another. I'll drink to that.

2 ounces water
2 ounces clear crème de menthe, divided
2½ ounces vodka, divided
Mint leaves for garnishing

YIELD: 1 COCKTAIL

1. Mix water, 1 ounce crème de menthe, and ½ ounce vodka.
2. Place a mint leaf in each of 4 wells of an ice cube tray. Pour the drink mixture into the 4 wells, distributing evenly.
3. Freeze overnight or until the ice cubes are fully frozen and release easily.
4. Chill a martini glass in the freezer.
5. Place the remaining 2 ounces vodka and 1 ounce crème de menthe in a shaker filled with regular ice. Shake until the shaker is evenly chilled.
6. Fill a martini glass with the four cocktail ice cubes, and then strain the shaker into the glass.

Rum Tum Tonic

Inspired by *Cats* (1982)

Cats: one of the most divisive musicals. Whether you love it or hate it, we can all agree on one thing: Rum Tum Tugger is an unforgettable character—and there's no doin' anything about it. Enjoy this bold dark rum drink in his honor. It's full of cream for your inner cat and striped like Tugger himself. Meow.

2 tablespoons white chocolate chips
Chocolate sprinkles for the rim
2 ounces dark rum
1 ounce coffee liqueur
1 ounce heavy whipping cream

YIELD: 1 COCKTAIL

1. Melt the white chocolate chips on a small plate by microwaving for 30 seconds and stirring. If not fully melted, microwave for another 30 seconds. Place the martini glass upside down on the plate, covering the rim in melted white chocolate. Then dip the rim into a plate of chocolate sprinkles until the rim is covered.
2. Pour the liqueur into the martini glass.
3. Shake the dark rum in a shaker full of ice. Strain into the martini glass above the liqueur. The rum should naturally sit on top of—not blend into—the liqueur.
4. Float the heavy cream on top of the rum.
5. Serve striped, but before drinking, give the glass a quick stir to combine the ingredients.

The Amazing Technicolor Dream Throat

Inspired by *Joseph and the Amazing Technicolor Dreamcoat* (1982)

Poor, poor, Joseph. What'cha gonna do if you're cast in the titular role, and you wake up with no voice the morning of your Broadway debut? Mix up this color-changing throat remedy, of course! One sip of this, and you'll feel well enough to make all your dreams come true.

2 slices ginger root
1 tablespoon dried butterfly pea flower
1½ ounces whiskey (optional)
½ tablespoon honey
Juice of 1 wedge lemon

YIELD: 1 DRINK

1. Place the ginger root and butterfly pea flower in a tea strainer.
2. Place the tea strainer in a mug, add the whiskey (if using), and fill with 2 cups hot water. Let steep for 1 minute.
3. Add the honey. Squeeze a lemon wedge into the mug, and watch the color change from blue to purple!
4. Drink up and let your cast members know you're on vocal rest until your big number.

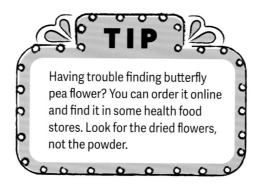

TIP

Having trouble finding butterfly pea flower? You can order it online and find it in some health food stores. Look for the dried flowers, not the powder.

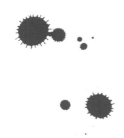

The Wizard and Ice

Inspired by *Wicked* (2003)

Toast everyone's favorite wicked witch with this cocktail inspired by the Wizard's green elixir. A few sips of this absinthe-based cocktail will make you feel like you're defying gravity. Don't let anyone bring you down—enjoy your moment with the Wizard and Ice.

1 glass crushed ice
4 mint leaves
½ ounce simple syrup
1½ ounces absinthe (the green stuff)
Juice of 1 wedge lime
6 to 8 ounces club soda
Mint sprig for garnishing
Lime twist for garnishing

YIELD: 1 COCKTAIL

1. Fill a collins glass with crushed ice. Set aside.
2. Muddle the mint leaves and simple syrup in the bottom of a shaker.
3. Add some ice, the absinthe, and the juice of the lime wedge to the shaker. Shake and strain into the collins glass.
4. Fill the rest of the glass with club soda, and garnish with a mint sprig and a lime twist.

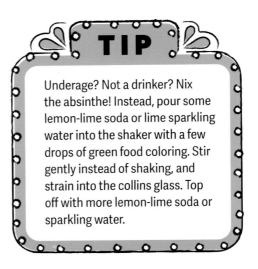

TIP

Underage? Not a drinker? Nix the absinthe! Instead, pour some lemon-lime soda or lime sparkling water into the shaker with a few drops of green food coloring. Stir gently instead of shaking, and strain into the collins glass. Top off with more lemon-lime soda or sparkling water.

Cuban Milkshake
Inspired by *Guys and Dolls* (1950)

Next time you're feeling pent up, whisk yourself off to Havana and indulge in a delicious Cuban Milkshake (or two). While some prefer to consider Bacardi the "flavoring" in this drink, we consider it the main event, with real dulce de leche and a pinch of cinnamon to round out the flavor. The result is guaranteed to ring your bell.

1½ ounces Bacardi Gold rum
1 ounce sweetened condensed milk
3 tablespoons dulce de leche
½ cup vanilla ice cream
½ cup ice cubes
Pinch ground cinnamon for garnishing

YIELD: 1 MILKSHAKE

1. Combine the rum, milk, dulce de leche, and vanilla ice cream in a blender with the ice cubes. Blend until thick and creamy.
2. Pour into a tall glass, and garnish with cinnamon.

TIP

Want to make your own dulce de leche? Pour a can of sweetened condensed milk into a double boiler, and cook over low heat for 40 to 50 minutes, until thick and caramel colored.

Substitute the rum for 1½ ounces milk to make a nonalcoholic milkshake. It's a great way to get kids to drink milk.

Sherry Baby

Inspired by *Jersey Boys* (2005)

Jersey Boys—a true story about a bunch of lovable scamps who formed a sensational band while finding themselves in and out of jail. The more you learn about them, the less you'd want Sherry to go out with them. But this red Sherry-inspired cocktail (complete with a twist) can make you like anyone just a bit more. With a few of these babies under your belt, you'll be ready to hit those Frankie Valli high notes at your nearest karaoke bar.

2 ounces amontillado sherry
½ ounce grenadine
½ ounce peach brandy
Juice of 1 lemon wedge
Lemon twist for garnishing
Maraschino cherry for garnishing

YIELD: 1 COCKTAIL

1. Combine the sherry, grenadine, peach brandy, and juice from the lemon wedge in a shaker with ice. Shake well.
2. Strain into a cocktail glass, and garnish with the lemon twist and maraschino cherry.

The Most Beautiful Thing
Inspired by *Kinky Boots* (2013)

We all remember falling in love with our first pair of bright red shoes. They're not meant to be practical; they're a work of art. You put them on, and they make you feel powerful. And your rear? Never looked better. This cocktail is inspired by Lola's dream shoe: a tall, glitzy, bright-red masterpiece. Now this is what a woman wants. Welcome to the kinky revolution!

Orange slice for rimming
Red sugar crystals for rimming
1 ounce pomegranate juice
1 ounce Cointreau
¼ teaspoon red edible pearl dust
Sparkling wine for topping

YIELD: 1 COCKTAIL

1. Rim the top of a champagne glass with an orange wedge, and dip into a plate of sugar crystals.
2. Add the pomegranate juice, Cointreau, pearl dust, and some ice to a shaker. Shake to mix.
3. Strain into the decorated champagne glass, and fill the rest of the glass with sparkling wine.

My Shot
Inspired by *Hamilton* (2015)

Hamilton is not just a moment, but a movement, and the characters inspire us all to take more shots. (Figuratively, that is.) Pick your favorite character and make a shot based on their pivotal moment from the show. You may be inspired to start your own revolution.

ALEXANDER:

Made with Caribbean rum and a hefty dose of coffee to keep you going nonstop.

YIELD: 1 LARGE SHOT

1 ounce Caribbean rum
½ ounce amaretto
1½ ounces black coffee
Whipped cream for topping

1. Pour the rum and amaretto into a large shot glass or rocks glass.
2. Carefully float the hot black coffee on top.
3. Top with whipped cream.

ELIZA:

Enough cinnamon to burn all the way down.

YIELD: 1 LARGE SHOT

2 ounces cinnamon whiskey
1 ounce alcoholic ginger beer

1. Combine the cinnamon whiskey and ginger beer in a shooter glass.

ANGELICA:

A take on a Brandy Alexander, guaranteed to satisfy.

YIELD: 1 LARGE SHOT

1 ounce Cognac
½ ounce crème de cacao
½ ounce heavy whipping cream

1. Add all ingredients to a shaker with ice.
2. Shake until combined and strain into a shooter glass.

AARON BURR:

Honey-infused bourbon. It takes a day to make, but sometimes if you want something to be good, you've gotta wait for it.

YIELD: 6 SHOTS

⅔ cup honey
½ cup water
1½ cups bourbon

1. Add the honey and water to a small saucepan over medium heat, and bring to a simmer. Simmer, stirring frequently, for 5 minutes to make simple syrup.
2. Combine the syrup and bourbon in a mason jar or bourbon jar. Close the jar, and shake to mix the honey and bourbon together.
3. Let sit overnight to allow flavors to meld.
4. Serve in shot glasses.

KING GEORGE:

Earl Grey–infused gin. It's not possible to get more British.

YIELD: 6 SHOTS

1½ cups gin
1 Earl Grey tea bag

1. Pour the gin into a mason jar, and add the tea bag. Let sit for 60 to 90 minutes or until as strong as you'd like.
2. Serve in shot glasses.

GEORGE WASHINGTON:

George Washington is going home . . . to make his own bourbon (shot).

YIELD: 1 SHOT

1 ounce bourbon
½ ounce sweet vermouth
1 drop grenadine

1. Pour the bourbon and vermouth into a shot glass, and add a drop of grenadine.

THOMAS JEFFERSON:

A Cognac shot that will make you wish you'd never left France.

YIELD: 1 LARGE SHOT

1½ ounces Cognac
1 ounce amaretto

1. Combine the ingredients in a shaker full of ice. Strain into a shot glass and shoot or sip.

Sunshine on the Shelf
Inspired by *Hadestown* (2019)

Winter can be hell. Just ask Persephone. Stuck in Hadestown every winter, she sneaks a bit of spring to the other inhabitants when the boss isn't looking. Keep your own batch of Sunshine on the Shelf for the next time those dark, gray days start to get to you down. Flavored with a burst of citrus, it will help remind you of the good old days of summer.

3 oranges
One 750-milliliter bottle vodka

YIELD: ONE 750-MILLILITER BOTTLE

1. Slice oranges.
2. Place orange slices in a 32-ounce wide-mouth mason jar.
3. Pour the vodka into the jar and seal.
4. Shake gently and keep in the fridge for at least 4 days or up to a month. Shake gently every 1 to 2 days.
5. Strain the vodka through a cheesecloth, and keep it in a bottle or jar. Discard the oranges.

Use the Sunshine on the Shelf to make Persephone's Pick-Me-Up, a cocktail that smells and tastes of spring:

2 ounces Sunshine on the Shelf
1 ounce sherry
½ ounce simple syrup
1 slice orange
1 sprig mint

YIELD: 1 COCKTAIL

1. Fill a shaker with ice, Sunshine, sherry, and simple syrup. Shake until chilled.
2. Pour into a rocks glass filled with ice. Garnish with an orange slice and mint sprig.

5

ENCORE

DESSERTS

• •

A truly great performance wouldn't be complete
without a dazzling encore. End the night on
a sweet note with these delectable desserts.
You're guaranteed to have your audience singing
your praises for the rest of the night.

• •

Laurey's Prize-Winning Tarts

Inspired by *Oklahoma!* (1943)

Want the farmers and the cowmen to fight over your picnic hamper at the annual auction? Better make sure you include a delicious tart. In *Oklahoma!*, Laurey makes her signature gooseberry tarts, but gooseberries can be difficult to find. However, mix together some strawberries (Oklahoma's state fruit) and some rhubarb, and you'll have a delicious treat that fits the same flavor profile. So good a cowman would give up his own saddle for a chance to enjoy them with you!

SHELLS
¾ cups all-purpose flour
¼ teaspoon salt
2 tablespoons shortening
2 tablespoons cold unsalted butter
2 tablespoons cold water

FILLING
2 cups chopped rhubarb
¼ cup sugar
2 tablespoons orange juice
1 cup diced strawberries
1 tablespoon cornstarch
½ teaspoon vanilla
Whipped cream for topping

TIP

Using premade shells? That's OK with us! Skip to step 5.
Pair with some meat pies and homemade jelly for an auction-winning hamper!

YIELD: 12 TARTS

1. To make the shells: Combine the flour and salt in a large bowl, then cut in the shortening and butter using a pastry blender or your hands. Add the cold water slowly, mixing until a dough forms.
2. Mold the dough into a flat disc, wrap in plastic wrap, and chill in the refrigerator for 30 minutes.
3. Take the dough out of the fridge and place on a lightly floured surface. Roll out the dough, and then fold it in half and then in half again. Roll out and fold the dough once more, then wrap and chill for another 30 minutes.
4. Preheat the oven to 350°F. Roll out the dough to ⅛ inch thick, and cut rounds with a 4-inch biscuit cutter. Turn a muffin tin upside down and spray the tin with cooking spray. Wrap each round of dough over the back of each muffin cup to form cup shapes. Place the tin with the dough in the oven (still upside down), and bake for 30 minutes. Remove and let cool for 5 minutes, then lift the shells off the tin and let cool on a wire rack while you make the filling.
5. To make the filling: In a medium saucepan, mix the rhubarb, sugar, and orange juice, and bring to a boil over medium heat. Reduce the heat till the mixture is just simmering, and simmer uncovered for 5 minutes or until the rhubarb has softened. Add the strawberries, cornstarch, and vanilla, and stir to combine. Cook for another 5 minutes, until strawberries have softened and the mixture has thickened. Let cool.
6. Fill each tart shell with the strawberry rhubarb mixture, and top with whipped cream.

Señorita Lolita Banana Flambé

Inspired by *Damn Yankees* (1955)

Whatever Señorita Lolita Banana wants, she gets. And when the temptress wants you, it's almost impossible to say no. This dessert is the fiery, boozy, sweet, and spicy version of Lola—and the devil knows it's hard to pass up once it's in front of you. Will you be able to resist the temptation?

1 tablespoon coconut oil
2 tablespoons brown sugar
½ teaspoon vanilla
¼ teaspoon ground cinnamon
¼ teaspoon ground nutmeg
2 bananas, peeled and halved lengthwise
1 ounce rum

YIELD: 2 SERVINGS

1. Melt coconut oil in a medium sauté pan over medium heat. Add the brown sugar, vanilla, cinnamon, and nutmeg, and stir. Let cook for 30 seconds or until the contents are fragrant.
2. Add the bananas, and cook for 1 minute on each side, until browned and coated in spices.
3. Remove the pan from the stove. Pour in the rum, and light a torch lighter right above the pan until the rum catches on fire. Let the rum fire burn off.
4. Serve the banana flambé with ice cream in a bowl or rimmed plate.

TIP

You are not the actual devil. Please be careful around fire. Make sure the pan is sitting on a heat resistant surface away from the stove and any open containers of liquor. Using a torch lighter instead of matches will prevent you from being too close to the flame. Have a fire extinguisher on hand, just in case!

Loverly Chocolate Truffles

Inspired by *My Fair Lady* (1956)

Eliza Doolittle just wants the simple things in life: A warm room, an enormous chair, and lots of chocolate. Well, with this simple recipe, she can have all the extravagant chocolate truffles she can eat. These decadent treats include Goldschläger and edible gold leaf, giving them a sophisticated finish. Too fair of a lady for alcohol in your chocolates? Leave it out and add a teaspoon of cinnamon instead.

¾ cup heavy whipping cream
24 ounces semisweet chocolate chips
2 tablespoons Goldschläger
Edible gold leaf or gold sprinkles for topping

TIP

Want these to look like something from a candy shop? Get a chocolate mold! Place the melted chocolate in a thin layer on the bottom of the molds, and move it around until the surface of the mold is completely coated. Let harden, press the chilled truffle mixture into the mold, filling it three quarters of the way, and then top with more melted chocolate. Chill in the fridge until hardened, and then pop the chocolates out of the mold.

YIELD: APPROXIMATELY 30 CHOCOLATES

1. In a medium saucepan, heat the cream over medium-low heat until simmering.
2. Turn off the stove, and slowly add 12 ounces of semisweet chocolate chips. Stir until the chocolate has melted and the mixture is smooth, about a minute. Add in the Goldschläger, and continue stirring until thoroughly mixed.
3. Pour the chocolate mixture onto a wax paper–lined pie plate or into a shallow casserole dish. Place in the fridge to chill for 1 hour or until firm but scoopable.
4. Remove the plate from the fridge, and scoop out an overflowing teaspoon of truffle filling. Roll into a ball, and place on a wax paper–covered plate. Repeat with the rest of the chocolate. Chill truffle balls in the fridge for 30 minutes.
5. Heat the other 12 ounces of chocolate in a double boiler on medium until the chocolate is melted and smooth, stirring often.
6. Pull the truffle balls out of the fridge, and dip into the melted chocolate, fully coating each truffle. Place the dipped chocolates on a wax paper–lined plate or cookie sheet, and top with a small piece of edible gold leaf or some gold sprinkles. Allow to harden completely before eating.

Officer Krupcakes

Inspired by *West Side Story* (1957)

While the Jets have some issues of their own they should be attending to, they instead blow off some steam with a long number making fun of the local police sergeant, Officer Krupke. It provides a bit of fun comic relief for the audience before *West Side Story* continues through its tragic end. In honor of poor Officer Krupke, we're making some cupcakes that an old-fashioned cop would surely enjoy: coffee-flavored, with a donut on top.

CUPCAKES

4 tablespoons instant coffee powder
1½ cups whole milk
2 cups all-purpose flour
2 cups sugar
1 cup unsweetened cocoa powder
1 teaspoon baking soda
1 teaspoon baking powder
½ teaspoon kosher salt
⅔ cup cooking oil
2 teaspoons vanilla
2 eggs

CREAM FILLING

½ cup shortening
½ cup unsalted butter
4 cups powdered sugar
1 teaspoon vanilla extract
2 tablespoons whole milk

BUTTERCREAM FROSTING

3 cups unsalted butter
6 cups powdered sugar
2 teaspoons vanilla
¼ teaspoon kosher salt

TOPPING

24 donut holes or mini donuts

YIELD: 24 CUPCAKES

1. To make the cupcakes: Preheat oven to 350°F, and prepare cupcake pans with liners (navy liners will bring in the color of the cops' uniforms).
2. In a small bowl, mix the instant coffee powder into the milk. Set aside.
3. In a large mixer bowl, sift together the flour, sugar, cocoa powder, baking soda, baking powder, and salt. Add the coffee mixture, oil, and vanilla.
4. Mix on low speed until combined, then mix on medium speed for 2 minutes. Add eggs one at a time, mixing between each egg, and then mix for 2 minutes more.
5. Fill each liner halfway with the cupcake mixture.
6. Bake for 22 minutes or until toothpick inserted in the center of a cupcake comes out clean. Let cool in the pans for 5 minutes, and then move to wire racks to cool completely.
7. To make the cream filling: Cream together the shortening and butter in a mixer until smooth. Add the powdered sugar ½ cup at a time, making sure each ½ cup is thoroughly incorporated before adding the next. Add the vanilla and milk, and mix for 2 minutes or until the mixture is light and fluffy. Transfer to a pastry bag with a small pastry tip at the end.
8. Scoop a small circle of cake from the top center of each cupcake. Fill each hole with the cream filling.
9. To make the buttercream frosting: Beat the unsalted butter in a mixer until light and fluffy. Slowly add the powdered sugar, ½ cup at a time, mixing fully each time. Add the vanilla and salt, and mix for 2 minutes or until you have a light, fluffy, thick buttercream frosting. Transfer the frosting to a pastry bag with a large pastry tip at the end.
10. Frost each cupcake, and top each with a donut hole or mini donut.

Coffee Break Cake

Inspired by
How to Succeed in Business Without Really Trying (1961)

It may sound extreme, but those with a daily nine-to-five know that sometimes the only thing keeping you going is your next coffee break. Sweeten up your next break with this Coffee Break Cake, inspired by recipes from the 1950s with an extra layer of cinnamon and spice in the middle. Bake it up and bring it into the office—it'll absolutely help you climb that corporate ladder.

CAKE

2 tablespoons sugar plus ½ cup
1 teaspoon ground cinnamon
¼ teaspoon ground nutmeg
¼ teaspoon ground ginger
2 tablespoons melted unsalted butter
½ cup half and half
1 egg
1 teaspoon vanilla
1 cup all-purpose flour
½ teaspoon kosher salt
2 teaspoons baking powder

STREUSEL TOPPING

1 tablespoon brown sugar
¼ teaspoon cinnamon
2 tablespoons flour
1 tablespoon salted butter, cold and cubed

YIELD: 9 SLICES OF COFFEE CAKE

1. Preheat the oven to 350°F, and butter an 8-by-8-inch square baking pan.
2. To make the cake: Combine 2 tablespoons sugar, cinnamon, nutmeg, and ginger in a small bowl and set aside.
3. In a medium bowl, mix the melted butter, ½ cup sugar, half and half, egg, and vanilla until egg is fully beaten.
4. Sift together the flour, salt, and baking powder, and add to the wet ingredients. Mix until thoroughly combined.
5. Spread half the cake batter evenly along the bottom of the pan, and then sprinkle the spice mixture evenly on top. Spread the remaining cake batter on top of that.
6. To make the streusel topping: Combine the brown sugar, cinnamon, flour, and butter. Pinch the topping with your hands to turn it into clumps and crumbles. Sprinkle the topping evenly on top of the cake batter.
7. Bake for 30 minutes or until a toothpick inserted in the cake comes out clean.
8. Let cool and cut into squares. Serve with a steaming cup of strong coffee.

A Pineapple Parfait for You

Inspired by *Cabaret* (1966)

They say diamonds are a girl's best friend, but a pineapple can mean a lot more. Especially in 1931 Berlin, when they're rare and very expensive. Share this delicious pineapple parfait with someone you love. Truly, you couldn't please them more.

1 cup heavy whipping cream
3 tablespoons powdered sugar
One 20-ounce can crushed pineapple
1 pint vanilla ice cream
2 graham crackers, crushed
2 maraschino cherries

YIELD: 2 PARFAITS

1. Place the whipping cream in a chilled mixer bowl with a whisk attachment, and start whisking on low. Slowly add the powdered sugar and 1 tablespoon of juice from the can of crushed pineapple. Slowly transition to whisking on high until medium peaks begin to form. Set aside.
2. Drain the can of crushed pineapple.
3. Place a scoop of ice cream at the bottom of each of two parfait cups.
4. Top the ice cream with 2 tablespoons crushed pineapple, then a tablespoon crushed graham cracker crumbs, then a scoop of pineapple whipped cream.
5. Repeat the process with another scoop of ice cream, followed by the pineapple, graham cracker crumbs, and whipped cream. Top each final scoop of whipped cream with a maraschino cherry.

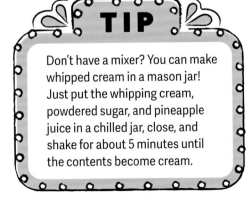

TIP

Don't have a mixer? You can make whipped cream in a mason jar! Just put the whipping cream, powdered sugar, and pineapple juice in a chilled jar, close, and shake for about 5 minutes until the contents become cream.

Sandy Dees
Inspired by *Grease* (1972)

Poor Sandy. She has her morals, and that just won't fly at her new school. While Sandy decides if she should stay straightlaced and demure or don a leather jacket and new 'do, we suggest you make an afternoon snack of these cookies, a take on a classic sandie, based on the pure, sweet, and uncomplicated version of Sandy we see at the beginning of the show. Add some pastel-colored sprinkles and white chocolate to give it a bit of flair, but don't forget: Sandy is "too pure to be pink."

1 cup unsalted butter, softened
¼ cup sugar
1 teaspoon vanilla
Dash kosher salt
2 cups all-purpose flour
2 cups pecans, finely chopped
White and yellow sprinkles for topping
12 ounces white chocolate chips
2 drops yellow food coloring or to desired color

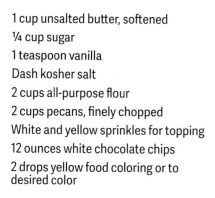

YIELD: 36 COOKIES

1. Preheat the oven to 350°F, and cover a cookie sheet with parchment paper.
2. Mix together the butter and sugar until smooth. Add the vanilla and salt and mix. Slowly add in the flour, pecans, and sprinkles until everything is thoroughly combined.
3. Shape cookie dough into 1-inch balls. Place 1 inch apart on the cookie sheet, and press down lightly on each cookie to flatten it.
4. Bake 11 to 14 minutes or until very lightly browned. Let cool on the baking sheet for 5 minutes, and then move to a wire rack to cool completely.
5. Melt the white chocolate chips by microwaving in a small bowl for 30 seconds at a time, stirring in between. Once melted, stir in a couple drops of yellow food coloring until you make a pastel yellow. Dip half of each cookie into the melted chocolate, and let harden on wax paper.

Angel (of Music) Food Cake

Inspired by *The Phantom of the Opera* (1988)

Christine is hearing voices again, and this time they're telling her to get to the kitchen and make some sweet Angel (of Music) Food Cake. This opera-cake-style dessert is made with angel food cake soaked in a hazelnut liqueur syrup, strawberry buttercream and jam, and a chocolate glaze. Now that is guaranteed to bring down the chandelier.

CAKE

¼ cup powdered sugar
½ cup all-purpose flour
1 tablespoon cornstarch
6 egg whites
¾ teaspoon cream of tartar
1 teaspoon vanilla
½ teaspoon kosher salt
½ cup sugar

HAZELNUT LIQUEUR SYRUP

1 cup sugar
1 cup water
⅓ cup hazelnut liqueur

STRAWBERRY BUTTERCREAM

½ cup unsalted butter
½ teaspoon vanilla
⅛ teaspoon salt
½ cup strawberry jam, divided
2 cups powdered sugar

CHOCOLATE GLAZE

¾ cup (about 6 ounces) semisweet chocolate chips
½ cup unsalted butter

YIELD: 6 SLICES

1. To make the cake: Preheat the oven to 325°F, and set an ungreased loaf pan aside. (The cake needs to stick to the pan, so there's no need to grease or line it with anything.)
2. Sift together the powdered sugar, flour, and cornstarch in a small bowl. Set aside.
3. Place the egg whites, cream of tartar, vanilla, and salt in a mixer bowl with a whisk attachment. Whisk on high for 30 seconds.
4. Slowly add in the sugar while continuing to whisk the egg white mixture. Whisk on low until sugar is incorporated, and then high until stiff peaks begin to form.
5. Using a spatula, fold the flour mixture into the egg whites until thoroughly combined.
6. Place the batter in the loaf pan, spreading evenly. Bake for 35 to 40 minutes or until lightly browned.
7. To cool, turn pan upside down, and balance the handles of the loaf pan on two equal-height cans or jars. Cool this way for 1 hour. While cooling, make the various fillings.
8. To make the hazelnut liqueur syrup: Combine the sugar and water in a small saucepan on medium heat. Heat, stirring often, until the sugar has dissolved and the mixture has thickened, about 4 to 5 minutes. Remove from heat. Add the liqueur and stir.

Continued on page 100

9. To make the strawberry buttercream: Beat the stick of unsalted butter in a mixer until smooth and creamy. Add vanilla, salt, and ¼ cup of jam and mix on high until light and fluffy, about two minutes. Add the powdered sugar one cup at a time, mixing in between to combine. Mix everything for about 5 minutes.

10. Run a butter knife around the inner edges of the pan to loosen the cake. Carefully remove the cake, and place on a cutting board. Slice thin horizontal layers, about ½ inch tall.

11. Create the cake: Place one layer of cake on a plate, then brush it with the hazelnut liqueur syrup. Spread half of the strawberry buttercream on top of the syrupy cake layer, and then top with another layer of cake. Brush the second layer with the syrup, spread a layer of the remaining strawberry jam, and then place a final layer of cake on top. Repeat once more with the syrup and the other half of the buttercream. Refrigerate for 30 minutes to cool and firm up.

12. To make the chocolate glaze: Melt the chocolate with the butter in a double boiler over medium heat, stirring until fully mixed and smooth.

13. Remove the cake from the fridge. Pour the glaze on top, and use a knife to spread it to the edges, creating a smooth, even layer. Place back in the refrigerator until the glaze is set, approximately 1 hour. Trim the edges of the cake to remove any spilled drips of glaze and reveal the gorgeous layers. Cut into 6 even slices and serve.

Honey, Honey

Inspired by *Mamma Mia* (2001)

1979: What a night. I made loukoumades, a traditional Greek dessert of fried donut holes soaked in honey, and well, let's just say they were as good as "dot, dot, dot." This is the one. I know it is. I've never felt like this before. Honey, Honey is my new go-to treat.

Two 2¼-teaspoon packets active dry yeast

1 cup warm water

1 cup warm whole milk

2 tablespoons sugar

1 teaspoon kosher salt

1 teaspoon vanilla

3½ cups flour

¾ cup honey

1 tablespoon water

Vegetable oil for frying plus more for scooping

2 teaspoons cinnamon

Toasted sesame seeds for topping (optional)

YIELD: 35 LOUKOUMADES

1. Mix together the yeast and warm water, and let sit for 5 minutes or until it begins to appear foamy.
2. In the bowl of your stand mixer, mix the milk, sugar, salt, and vanilla. Once combined, add the yeast mixture, and continue to mix. Slowly mix in the flour one cup at a time until a dough forms.
3. Cover the mixing bowl, and let rise for 1 hour or until doubled in size.
4. Heat the honey and 1 tablespoon water in a small saucepan over medium-high heat for 5 minutes. Turn off the heat, and set aside to cool slightly.
5. Fill the bottom of a large, heavy pot or Dutch oven 2 inches deep with oil, and heat to 350°F.
6. Pour some vegetable oil in a bowl, and dip a spoon in the oil. Using the oily spoon, scoop up a spoonful of dough, round it slightly with your fingers, and drop it in the hot oil. Continue with the rest of the dough, careful not to overcrowd in the pot. Keep an eye on which dough balls went in first—you'll want to fry each ball for 2 to 3 minutes, turning to make sure all sides become golden. Place fried loukoumades on a large plate or baking sheet covered in paper towels to drain.
7. Move the fried loukoumades to a large serving plate, and cover them generously with the honey syrup. Sprinkle cinnamon and sesame seeds if using over the top and serve warm.

Big, Beautiful Blondie

Inspired by *Hairspray* (2002)

Watching *Hairspray* is like eating your favorite dessert: It leaves you feeling upbeat, gratified, and full of sugar. The song "Big, Blonde, and Beautiful" is a big part of that, leaving everyone feeling beautiful, empowered, and hungry thanks to all the food imagery. Enjoy these large pecan blondies with a chocolate swirl—the edible version of the sweet song.

Butter for greasing plus ½ cup
Flour for dusting plus 1 cup
½ teaspoon kosher salt
¾ cup brown sugar
1 egg
1½ teaspoons vanilla
½ cup chopped pecans
½ cup semisweet chocolate

YIELD: 9 BIG, BEAUTIFUL BLONDIES

1. Preheat the oven to 350°F, and butter an 8-by-8-inch baking pan. Dust with flour, and tap out the excess.
2. Combine the 1 cup flour and the salt in a small bowl. Set aside.
3. Add the butter and sugar to a large mixing bowl, and mix until combined. Add the egg and vanilla, and mix until fully combined.
4. Slowly add the flour mixture to the wet ingredients, and mix just until combined. Fold in the chopped pecans.
5. Spread the batter evenly in the baking pan.
6. Melt the chocolate by microwaving for 30 seconds at a time, stirring in between, until smooth.
7. Drizzle the melted chocolate in long lines across the batter. Swirl it by dragging a butter knife through the chocolate perpendicular to the line.
8. Bake for 25 minutes or until a toothpick inserted in the center comes out clean. Let cool on a wire rack, and then cut into nine equal giant blondies.
9. Enjoy the whole damn feast!

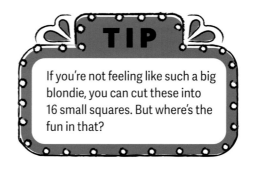

TIP

If you're not feeling like such a big blondie, you can cut these into 16 small squares. But where's the fun in that?

Piragua, Piragua

Inspired by *In the Heights* (2008)

May we all have the optimism and work ethic of the Piragua Guy. Selling his freshly shaved ice on the hottest days. Keeping everyone cool when the Mister Softee truck mysteriously breaks down. Even if you don't have a local piragua cart, you can make your own mango-strawberry version in your kitchen. Just don't try to open up your own stand. This is his town.

1 mango, peeled and pitted

5 large strawberries, stemmed

1 cup sugar

1 cup water

1 tablespoon lemon juice

2 cups ice cubes

YIELD: 1 PIRAGUA

1. Place mango, strawberries, sugar, water, and lemon juice in a blender. Blend until smooth.
2. Transfer the fruit mixture to a small pan and bring to a boil. Reduce to medium-low heat, and let simmer for 10 minutes.
3. Let the fruit syrup cool slightly, and then pour into a mason jar. Refrigerate until completely chilled.
4. Place ice cubes in a shaved ice maker or blender, and power until ice is fully crushed. Build the ice into a pyramid shape in a short cup or bowl.
5. Drizzle ¼ cup of fruit syrup around the sides and top of the ice pyramid. Serve with a spoon and straw.

Spooky Mormon Hell Cream Donut

Inspired by *The Book of Mormon* (2011)

Hello! Have you heard about the Book of Mormon? It may be the only thing that can save you from your own personal Spooky Mormon Hell Dream. If you don't happen to have a copy of the Book on hand, try sinking your teeth into one of these delectable donuts instead. Heck, man up and eat them two by two. They're almost as good as a visit to Orlando.

DONUT

One 2¼ package active dry yeast

½ cup warm water

½ cup warm whole milk

⅓ cup sugar

2 eggs

1 teaspoon kosher salt

½ cup unsalted butter, softened

4 cups bread flour

Canola oil for frying

CREAM FILLING

¼ cup shortening

¼ cup butter

2 cups powdered sugar

½ teaspoon vanilla extract

1 tablespoon whole milk

MAPLE GLAZE

2 cups powdered sugar

½ cup pure maple syrup

¼ teaspoon vanilla

¼ teaspoon kosher salt

1 tablespoon hot water

YIELD: 12 DONUTS

1. Whisk together the yeast, water, and milk, and let sit for 5 minutes or until foamy. Whisk in the sugar, eggs, and salt.

2. Add the flour to the wet ingredients one cup at a time, stirring until fully mixed each time. Cut in the softened butter, and mix until fully incorporated.

3. Knead the dough on a lightly floured cutting board for about 5 minutes. Place in a greased bowl, and cover with plastic wrap. Let sit until the dough doubles in size, about 90 minutes.

4. Punch down the dough, and form into a large rectangle on a floured surface. Roll out the dough into an 8-by-12-inch rectangle. Cut the dough into 12 small rectangular bars.

5. Move the bars onto a parchment paper–lined baking sheet, leaving ½ inch between each bar. Cover loosely with plastic wrap, and let rise for 1 hour.

6. Fill a large, heavy pot or Dutch oven with about 2 inches of canola oil, and heat to about 370°F. Carefully place the donuts into the oil, two at a time, and fry for 1 minute on each side or until browned. Remove with a spatula or tongs, and place fried donuts on paper towels to drain and cool.

7. In the meantime, make the cream filling: Cream together the shortening and butter in a mixer until smooth. Add the powdered sugar ½ cup at a time, making sure each ½ cup is completely incorporated before adding the next. Add the vanilla and milk, and mix for 2 minutes or until the mixture is light and fluffy. Transfer to a pastry bag with a small pastry tip at the end.

8. Make a small pocket in each donut by sticking a small, sharp knife through the middle of one of the edges. Insert the pastry tip into each pocket, and fill with the cream.

9. To make the maple glaze: Whisk the glaze ingredients together in a wide bowl until smooth. Dip the top of each donut into the glaze, and let excess flow back into the bowl. Turn the donut over, and place on a plate until the glaze has set, about 10 minutes. Dip donuts a second time for a more opaque glaze.

Sugar Daddy Honey Roll

Inspired by *Hedwig and the Angry Inch* (2014)

When Hedwig sings about dripping like a honeycomb, she's really just excited about eating a sticky, sweet honey roll—right? In any case, this Sugar Daddy Honey Roll, inspired by the lyrics of her song, her gorgeous golden curls, and her colorful makeup will make you want to sing.

DOUGH

1 cup all-purpose flour
1 teaspoon baking powder
¼ teaspoon kosher salt
3 eggs
1 cup sugar
⅓ cup cold water
2 teaspoons vanilla
Powdered sugar for dusting

HONEY WHIPPED CREAM FILLING

1 cup heavy whipping cream
3 tablespoons honey
½ teaspoon vanilla
⅛ teaspoon cinnamon
1 tablespoon rainbow sprinkles

TOPPINGS

Powdered sugar
Honey
Rainbow sprinkles

YIELD: 1 HONEY ROLL

1. To make the dough: Preheat the oven to 375°F. Line a jelly roll pan with parchment paper, then grease the paper and the sides of the pan.
2. Combine the flour, baking powder, and salt in a small bowl. Set aside.
3. In a large mixer, whisk the eggs on a medium speed until light yellow and frothy. Add the sugar, water, and vanilla, and mix until combined.
4. Add the dry ingredients to the wet ingredients and mix.
5. Pour the batter into the pan, making sure it spreads evenly to all edges. Bake for 10 to 12 minutes or until the cake springs back to a light touch.
6. Dust a clean dish towel with powdered sugar, and place the towel over the jelly roll pan, sugar side down. Flip so the cake is now resting on the towel. Remove the pan and parchment paper.
7. While the cake is still warm, gently roll it up with the towel to help it find its shape. Let the cake cool like this for 10 minutes.
8. In the meantime, make the honey whipped cream filling: Combine the whipping cream, honey, vanilla, and cinnamon in a chilled mixer bowl with a whisk attachment. Whisk on high speed until medium peaks form. Fold in 1 tablespoon of rainbow sprinkles.
9. Carefully unroll the cake, and spread the honey whipped cream filling on top. Roll up the cake. Top the roll with powdered sugar, drizzles of honey, and rainbow sprinkles.

Pomatter Pie

Inspired by *Waitress* (2016)

They say doctors are smart, but what smart person would willingly give up sugar? This delicious marshmallow crème pie is guaranteed to accidentally seduce even the most awkward ob-gyn. Get ready to fall in love—it only takes a taste.

1¼ cups all-purpose flour

½ teaspoon kosher salt

2½ tablespoons sugar, divided

½ cup cold unsalted butter, cubed

¼ cup cold water

4 cups mini marshmallows

5 cups heavy whipping cream, divided

8 ounces cream cheese

1½ teaspoons vanilla, divided

YIELD: 1 PIE (8 SLICES)

1. Combine the flour, salt, and ½ tablespoon sugar in a large bowl, then cut in the butter until you have a fully mixed and slightly crumbly dough.
2. Sprinkle some of the water over the dough mixture, and mix with your hands until the dough sticks together. If it's still crumbly, add a bit more water.
3. Form the dough into a ball, and then press into a disc. Wrap in plastic wrap and refrigerate for 1 hour.
4. Preheat the oven to 425°F.
5. Flour a large surface, and roll out the dough until it's 12 inches in diameter. Place in a pie pan and press down, crimping the edges.
6. Line the base of the crust with parchment paper, and pour marbles, dried beans, or pie weights on top of it. (This will prevent the crust from puffing up.) Bake the crust for 18 minutes or until golden brown and let cool.
7. Add the marshmallows and 1 cup cream to a medium saucepan over medium-high heat. Stir often until marshmallows are melted and thoroughly mixed with the cream, about three minutes. Remove from heat, and add in the cream cheese and 1 teaspoon vanilla. Mix, and then let cool.
8. Add 4 cups whipping cream, 2 tablespoons sugar, and ½ teaspoon vanilla to a chilled mixer bowl, and mix on high speed until peaks form.
9. Fold 2 cups of the whipped cream into the marshmallow mixture. Spread the mixture into the pie crust and refrigerate for 2 hours. Refrigerate the rest of the whipped cream as well.
10. Using a piping bag, pipe the rest of the whipped cream onto the pie. Serve with a stethoscope.

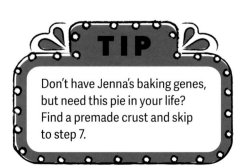

TIP

Don't have Jenna's baking genes, but need this pie in your life? Find a premade crust and skip to step 7.

A La Mode Sundae

Inspired by *Dear Evan Hansen* (2016)

When Evan describes his perfect day with Connor, we can taste the ice cream, feel the late-spring sun, and picture the sky that goes on for forever, even though we know his friendship and the day are complete lies. Live your own too good to be true day with this sundae inspired by A La Mode and the Autumn Smile Apple Orchard. Share it with a friend while you talk and take in the view—like buddies do.

CINNAMON SWIRL ICE CREAM
1 quart vanilla bean ice cream
¼ cup brown sugar
1 teaspoon cinnamon
2 tablespoons salted butter, melted

STEWED APPLES
1 tablespoon salted butter
2 apples, peeled, cored, and thinly sliced
¼ cup water
1 tablespoon brown sugar
¼ teaspoon ground cinnamon
¼ teaspoon ground ginger
¼ teaspoon ground allspice
¼ teaspoon ground nutmeg

TOPPINGS
Whipped cream
Chopped peanuts

YIELD: 2 SUNDAES

1. To make the cinnamon swirl ice cream: Take the ice cream out of the freezer, and transfer to a large bowl.
2. Combine the brown sugar, cinnamon, and melted butter in a small bowl. Fold into the ice cream, making swirls throughout the vanilla. Place the ice cream back into its quart container, and put back in the freezer.
3. To make the stewed apples: Place 1 tablespoon butter and the apple slices in a small saucepan on medium heat. Cook the apples for 4 minutes or until softened.
4. Add the water, brown sugar, and spices to the pot. Bring to a boil, and let apples stew for 5 minutes or until the liquid is reduced in half.
5. Place 2 scoops of ice cream in each of two bowls. Top with stewed apples, whipped cream, and nuts.

Revenge Party Cake

Inspired by *Mean Girls* (2018)

Cady Heron is about to serve the Plastics a taste of their own medicine, and she's going to do it with the help of this Revenge Party Cake. Decorated with candy canes and "bloody" red ganache, this pink peppermint cake tastes as sweet as revenge. Here's hoping you're not on an all-carb diet.

CAKE

2½ cups flour

2½ teaspoons baking powder

½ teaspoon kosher salt

¾ cup unsalted butter, room temperature

1½ cups sugar

3 eggs, room temperature

1½ teaspoons vanilla

2 teaspoons peppermint extract

1¼ cups whole milk

Pink gel food coloring

FROSTING LAYERS

3 cups unsalted butter, room temperature

6 cups powdered sugar

2 teaspoons vanilla

¼ teaspoon kosher salt

Pink gel food coloring

1 cup crushed crunchy chocolate mint cookies

GANACHE AND TOPPINGS

½ cup white candy melts, peppermint or vanilla flavored

¼ cup heavy whipping cream

Red gel food coloring

Candy canes for decorating

Red frosting writer for decorating

YIELD: 1 CAKE (8 SLICES)

1. To make the cake: Preheat the oven to 350°F. Grease and flour four 6-inch round pans.
2. Mix the flour, baking powder, and salt in a bowl. Set aside.
3. Beat the butter and sugar together in a mixer until light and fluffy. Add eggs to the butter mixture one at a time, mixing each one into the batter completely before adding the next. Mix in the vanilla and peppermint extract.
4. Add half of the dry ingredients to the wet mixture, and mix thoroughly. Add half of the milk, and mix thoroughly. Repeat with the rest of the dry ingredients, followed by the rest of the milk. Beat in the pink gel food coloring a couple drops at a time until you reach your preferred shade of pink.
5. Pour a quarter of the cake batter into each pan.
6. Bake for 25 to 30 minutes or until a toothpick inserted in the middle comes out clean. Cool for 10 minutes in the pan, and then remove the cakes from the pans and cool completely on wire racks.

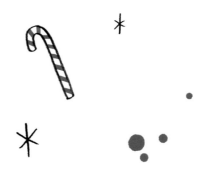

Continued on page 116

7. To make the frosting: Beat 3 cups of unsalted butter in a mixer until light and fluffy. Slowly add the powdered sugar, ½ cup at a time, mixing fully each time. Add the vanilla and salt, and mix for 2 minutes or until you have a light, fluffy, thick buttercream frosting.

8. Divide the frosting into two small bowls. In one bowl, add two drops of pink gel food coloring and mix. Continue adding food coloring a drop or two at a time until the frosting is the color of the Burn Book. Place the frosting into two separate piping bags with large pastry tips.

9. Slice the rounded top off of each cake layer so they're flat and even. Place one cake layer on a serving plate, and pipe white frosting around the top edge. Fill in the middle with white frosting, and spread lightly to make an even layer. Top with a second cake layer, and frost with the white frosting again.

10. Sprinkle crushed cookies on top of the second layer of frosting. Top with the third cake layer and another layer of white frosting, and then add the final cake layer.

11. Pipe a small amount of pink frosting along the edges and top of the cake, and spread evenly with a spatula to make a crumb coat.

12. Pipe pink frosting along all sides of the cake, starting at the bottom and working your way to the top. Frost the top of the cake. Using a spatula, gently work your way around the cake to spread the frosting into an even coating.

13. To make the "bloody" ganache: Melt the candy melts with the cream in a small saucepan on low, stirring often, or microwave in 15-second increments, stirring in between. Remove from heat, and add red gel food coloring until the ganache is blood-red.

14. Let cool and then place the bloody ganache in a squeeze bottle or pastry bag with a very small hole cut. Squeeze the ganache along the top edges of the cake, allowing it to drip down the sides.

15. Pipe large dots of the remaining white frosting around the top edges of the cake. In each dot, place a candy cane.

16. If you want, in the center of the cake, use a red frosting writer to write "fugly cow" or your own personal message of vengeance.

5

PARTY TIME!

· ·

Now that you've mastered the art of cooking
for Broadway, it's time to dress your set, finalize
your cues, and invite your friends over for a
production they'll never forget. Here are some
party ideas that incorporate Broadway-inspired
recipes with a few additional ideas for décor,
activities, and more!

· ·

Tony Awards Soirée

Tonight's the night! Celebrate the best of Broadway with your closest friends. Encourage everyone to dress up like they're expecting to win big at the Tonys, and break out your best black and silver décor. Black and silver balloons, metallic stars, and a red-carpet entrance will give your space some festive flair. If you have playbills or posters of the nominated shows, display them on your walls. Make sure everyone arrives right before the red-carpet coverage begins so they have plenty of time to fill out their ballots and bingo cards.

FOOD

- Set out Totally Shucked (page 28) and I Yam What I Yam (page 44) for your delightful amuse-bouches.
- During the show, serve Cheesy Street (page 20) with an assortment of dippers.
- Angel (of Music) Food Cake (page 98) makes for a beautiful dessert for the second half of the night.
- Package some Loverly Chocolate Truffles (page 91) in small boxes as party favors for your guests.

DRINKS

- The Most Beautiful Thing (page 81) is a drink made for the red carpet—sip it as you ooh and aah over your guests' fabulous outfits.
- Make a round of Another Vodka Stingers (page 72) right before the show starts. With your backup drink already melting in your glass, you won't have to miss a thing!

ACTIVITIES

- Download an official Tony Awards ballot, and cast your votes before the show starts. Keep score—winner gets a prize!
- Print out blank bingo boards, and have your guests fill in the squares with things they think will happen during the show. See who can get a bingo first! Possible options can include:
    - A shout-out to the "kids watching at home—this could be you!"
    - Stage actors making fun of TV and movie actors
    - Someone flubbing a line during their intro
    - A winner crying during a speech
    - A show winning more than six awards
- Hold your own awards ceremony at the end of the night, and give out fake Tonys to the ballot winner, the bingo winner, and the best dressed of the night.

MUSIC

- Put together the greatest hits from each nominated musical, and play them before the coverage begins.

Cast Party

You finished your final performance, and it's time to celebrate with your theater family! Get those cast shirts on, and get ready to sing, dance, and reminisce about your show's run all night long.

FOOD

- Start the night with some Don't Fry for Me, Argentina (page 23) empanadas—the cast will be hungry after their final show!
- Make up big bowls of Greens, Greens, Nothing but Greens (page 25) and either Age of Asparagus (page 57) or Mama's Well-Peppered Ragù (page 59), and set them out family style so everyone can help themselves throughout the night.
- Make Officer Krupcakes (page 92) and Big, Beautiful Blondies (page 104) in advance for some easy and delicious party treats.

DRINKS

- Recover from the show with Joseph and The Amazing Technicolor Dream Throats (page 75).
- Mix up a batch of Cuban Milkshakes (page 78) with or without the liquor for a fun treat. After all, you can finally have dairy again without worrying about your voice!
- Make a batch of bright-green Wizard and Ice (page 76) cocktails in honor of the green room you all spent too much time in.

ACTIVITIES

- Put together a list of unofficial awards to hand out to castmates during a silly ceremony. This is the time to incorporate all those inside jokes. Who gave the best backrubs? Who made everyone laugh backstage the most? Who had the most adoring fans in the audience? Who did everyone turn to for makeup help?
- Take a stack of your show's posters, and hang them up on your wall with the blank sides showing. Write a cast member's name on each poster, and encourage your guests to write memories and sweet messages to each other. Send the posters home with your guests as a fun memento.
- Have a recording of your performance? Put it on in the background.

MUSIC

- Take your show's music, and mix it in with some of the most singable Broadway hits. Everyone will be singing and dancing along before you know it. Some suggestions:
  - "Summer Nights," *Grease*
  - "Suddenly Seymour," *Little Shop of Horrors*
  - "Defying Gravity," *Wicked*
  - "All That Jazz," *Chicago*
  - "Seasons of Love," *Rent*
  - "One Day More," *Les Misérables*
  - "Can't Stop the Beat," *Hairspray*
  - "Memory," *Cats*
  - "You Will Be Found," *Dear Evan Hansen*
  - "A Whole New World," *Aladdin*

Prematinée Brunch

Heading to a matinée? Gather your friends for an extravagant brunch before the show! Have them arrive in their most dapper brunch attire—you'll be all set to walk into the theater dressed to impress. Decorate your place with fresh-cut flowers, and pull out your nicest plates and cloth napkins.

APPETIZERS

- Make these recipes the night before your guests arrive, and set out the spread right before your brunch begins. That way you and your guests will have something to munch on while you're finishing the main courses.
- In the mood for fruity? Make A Sunny Ball of Butter (page 40) and Lady Marmalade (page 48).
- Prefer savory? Make Along Came Bialy (page 26) and I'm Still Schmear (page 43), and pair with onions, capers, and lox.

MAIN DISHES

- Newfoundland Toutons (page 67). Set the finished toutons out on a serving plate with tongs, and surround with assorted toppings such as maple syrup, molasses, powdered sugar, freshly cut fruit, and whipped cream. Serve with the bacon you cooked for the recipe.
- Waiting for the Egg (page 18). Give each guest their own egg cup and plate of toast soldiers.

DRINKS

- Mix the Sunshine on the Shelf (page 85) infused vodka with orange juice for an extra-juicy screwdriver.
- Make a breakfast version of the Alexander Shot (page 82) by pouring it into a coffee cup and topping it off with extra coffee.

MUSIC

- Make a playlist of your favorite energizing Broadway songs about the morning and sun. Here are a few to get you started:
  - "Oh, What a Beautiful Mornin'," *Oklahoma!*
  - "Good Morning," *Singin' in the Rain*
  - "Good Morning Baltimore," *Hairspray*
  - "Let the Sunshine In," *Hair*
  - "Don't Rain on My Parade," *Funny Girl*
  - "Morning Person," *Shrek the Musical*
  - "Seize the Day," *Newsies*
  - "Opening Up," *Waitress*
  - "Put on Your Sunday Clothes," *Funny Girl*
  - "Bikini Bottom Day," *SpongeBob SquarePants: The Musical*

Curtain Call: Acknowledgments

A huge thank you to my leading man, Alexander Theoharis. You support my crazy ideas and passions, even when it results in me doing nothing but watching and listening to Broadway performances for months on end. You're my best friend and the love of my life, and I'm so lucky to get to spend every day with you.

Thank you to my supporting ladies, Makenzie Greenblatt and Satabdi Chakrabarti, for always being there to cheer me on and keep me "sane," even when they're busy being the stars of their own lives. I cherish the time we get to spend together, singing along to our favorite musicals and making stupid jokes no one else would laugh at. (And thank you for putting up with me, even though I sing off-key next to your beautiful voices!)

Thank you to Brandon Ivie for all your Broadway wisdom and excellent recipe suggestions. Thank you to Rhonda Miller and Kristina Horner for your advice on specific recipes and how to make them even more authentic and delicious. Thank you to Drew Barth, Zachary Cohn, Katrina Hamilton, Meagan LaBrasseur, and Danielle Sparks for your puntastic assistance with the recipe titles.

I had a full ensemble of recipe testers that helped make sure these recipes work for everyone: Julia Bokma Parker, Mary Byers, Kaelin Carson, Zachary Cohn, Abbey Conroy, Gabe Conroy, Jenn Godwin, Justin Hammond, Tally Heilke, Joe Homes, David Hudson, Jordon Huppert, Sarah Huppert, Joe Kim, Elizabeth Marcus Moore, Chris Parker, Danielle Sparks, Andreas Theoharis, Roni Theoharis, Gavin Verhey, Lauryl Zenobi, and David Zimmermann. Thank you all!

And thank you so much to my editor, Hilary VandenBroek, my agent Maria Vicente, and everyone at Insight Editions for being as excited about this idea as I am and helping me bring it to life. This wouldn't have happened without all of you.

About the Author

Tara Theoharis is the creator of the Geeky Hostess, a fandom-inspired recipe and party site, and the author of *The Minecrafter's Cookbook*. She's been a musical-theater lover ever since she saw Rodgers and Hammerstein's *Cinderella* live as a kid and became a certified Renthead starting with the show's first national tour. In addition to *Cinderella* and *Rent*, her favorite shows include *Guys and Dolls, Bye Bye Birdie, Little Shop of Horrors, Legally Blonde*, and *Hamilton*. She's been a proud ensemble member, quietly singing in the back, for community and high school productions of *Joseph and the Amazing Technicolor Dreamcoat, Annie, Brigadoon, Oklahoma!*, and *The Pajama Game*.

INSIGHT EDITIONS

PO Box 3088
San Rafael, CA 94912
www.insighteditions.com

Find us on Facebook: www.facebook.com/InsightEditions
Follow us on Twitter: @insighteditions

Library of Congress Cataloging-in-Publication Data available.

ISBN: 978-1-68383-883-8

Publisher: Raoul Goff
President: Kate Jerome
Associate Publisher: Vanessa Lopez
Creative Director: Chrissy Kwasnik
VP of Manufacturing: Alix Nicholaeff
Designer: Judy Wiatrek Trum
Editor: Hilary VandenBroek
Editorial Assistant: Anna Wostenberg
Managing Editor: Lauren LePera
Production Editor: Jennifer Bentham
Production Manager: Eden Orlesky

Illustrations by Neryl Walker
Photography by Ted Thomas
Food and Prop Styling: Elena P. Craig
Food and Prop Styling Assistant: Wesley Anderson

Special thanks to Daliah Neuberger, Orah Neuberger Sholin, Neville Vania, Megan Sinead Harris, and Hilary Thomas.

ROOTS of PEACE   REPLANTED PAPER

Insight Editions, in association with Roots of Peace, will plant two trees for each tree used in the manufacturing of this book. Roots of Peace is an internationally renowned humanitarian organization dedicated to eradicating land mines worldwide and converting war-torn lands into productive farms and wildlife habitats. Roots of Peace will plant two million fruit and nut trees in Afghanistan and provide farmers there with the skills and support necessary for sustainable land use.

Manufactured in China by Insight Editions

10 9 8 7 6 5 4 3 2